Marble Collectors Handbook

 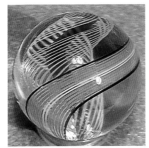 

Robert S. Block

4880 Lower Valley Road, Atglen, PA 19310 USA

Dedication

This book is dedicated to marble collectors everywhere, who have turned a childhood game into a full-fledged hobby, and to my wife, Sarah, and children, Kevin, Benjamin, and Nathaniel, the lights of my life.

Published by Schiffer Publishing Ltd.
4880 Lower Valley Road
Atglen, PA 19310
Phone: (610) 593-1777; Fax: (610) 593-2002
E-mail: Info@schifferbooks.com

Copyright © 2005 by Robert S. Block
Library of Congress Control Number: 2005924629

Designed by Mark David Bowyer
Type set in Americana XBd BT/Souvenir Lt BT

ISBN: 0-7643-2331-8
Printed in China

For the largest selection of fine reference books on this and related subjects, please visit our web site at
www.schifferbooks.com
We are always looking for people to write books on new and related subjects. If you have an idea for a book please contact us at the above address.

This book may be purchased from the publisher.
Include $3.95 for shipping.
Please try your bookstore first.
You may write for a free catalog.

In Europe, Schiffer books are distributed by
Bushwood Books
6 Marksbury Ave.
Kew Gardens
Surrey TW9 4JF England
Phone: 44 (0) 20 8392-8585; Fax: 44 (0) 20 8392-9876
E-mail: info@bushwoodbooks.co.uk
Free postage in the U.K., Europe; air mail at cost.

CONTENTS

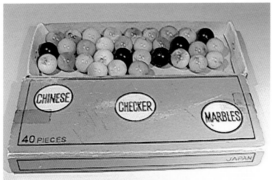

ACKNOWLEDGMENTS

No book is written solely by the author. There were a number of other people who contributed in various ways to what you are holding in your hands.

All of the photos in this book are of marbles that have been sold in Block's Box, A Chip Off The Old Block or The AuctionBlocks auctions, or are from the author's collection.

My thanks to David Tamulevich and Dennis Webb for sharing their research on Alley Agate Company, Heaton Agate Company, JABO Inc., and Cairo Novelty Company.

Thanks also to my wife, Sarah, for her unending support.

A special thanks to Peter Schiffer and his staff, for their superb support during this project.

INTRODUCTION

This book is an adjunct to my *Marbles: Identification and Price Guide*. That book, as with almost all marble books currently in print, list the author's best estimate of the average value of average examples. The actual price of a marble depends on a number of factors. In a perfect marketplace, the actual value of a marble would be determined by rarity, size, and condition. Those factors are fairly objective and can be quantified with relative ease by any collector with a little practice and experience. But, every marble is different (they are not a commodity item), and the antique and collectible marketplace is inherently imperfect. The price of a marble at any particular point in time is determined by factors other than rarity, size, and condition. The value is also determined by eye appeal and the emotions of the persons trying to purchase and sell it. This book reports the actual prices realized for actual, individual marbles.

This book analyzes the actual realized prices for over 22,000 separate and individual marbles. The price record covers every individual marble sold in A Chip Off The Old Block's and The AuctionBlocks marble auctions for a two-year period ending August 31, 2004.

A full range of handmade, machine made, and contemporary marbles, as well as marble packages and other related items, are covered in this book. For handmade and machine made marbles, there is a table provided for each individual marble type. This lists by size range, and by condition range, several statistics for that marble type. These include:

High: The highest price realized for that size and condition range
Low: The lowest price realized for that size and condition range
Average: The statistical mean for all marbles of that type in that size and condition
  range
Quantity: The number of marbles included in the Average

In some cases, where the highest or lowest priced marble in that particular cell of the table was not representative of the other prices, the price was discarded. For example, if there was a Peltier Peerless Patch that was 5/8" and in 9.7 condition, that sold for 50¢, and all other Peltier Peerless Patches sold for between $2.00 and $32.00, then the 50¢ marble was not considered representative of the group and was not included in the totals. The same procedure was used for any marbles that sold significantly higher than the range. This elimination of "outliers" will hopefully produce a better view of the price of specific marbles.

The price tables for contemporary marbles are somewhat different. Since almost all contemporary marbles are close to 9.9, there were no marbles included in the tables that were graded lower than 9.7. Also, while each artist may produce many different designs, they each generally only utilize one technique. Prices for each artist are reported by size range.

There are no price tables for marble packages and marble related items, due to their relative rarity. I have illustrated about 150 representative examples with their selling prices.

This book is designed to complement and be used in conjunction with *Marbles: Identification and Price Guide*. The layout of marble types and subcategories in this book is virtually identical to that in *MIPG*. While *MIPG* provides idealized prices for each cell of the table, this book provides a look at actual prices realized. You can use the high, low, and average prices in this book with the Multiplier guidelines in *MIPG* to estimate the value of virtually any marble. My hope is that this book will be useful to you in valuing your own collection, or in pursuing the hobby of marble collecting.

VALUING MARBLES

There are four factors that determine the value of a marble: Type, Condition, Size and Eye Appeal. The most important determinant of marble value is the rarity of the type. Generally, marbles are classified into the following categories:

Handmade Glass (categorized by design)
Cane-cut or Rod-cut
  Swirl
        Latticinio core
        Divided (or Open) core
        Solid core
        Ribbon core
        Joseph's Coat
        Banded (or coreless)
        Miscellaneous core
        Peppermint
        Clambroth
        Banded Opaque
        Indian
        Banded lutz
        Ribbon lutz
        Indian lutz
        Miscellaneous swirls
  End of Day
        Cloud
        Onionskin
        Panelled onionskin
        Joseph Coat
        Mist
        Indian
        Banded opaque
        Submarine
        End of day onionskin lutz
        Mist lutz
        Indian Lutz
  Miscellaneous
        Mica
        Slag
        Opaque
        Clearie

Single-gather
　Sulphide
　Cloud
　Mica
　Paperweight

Handmade Non-Glass
Clay
　Clay
　Bennington
　Crockery
　Stoneware
　China
　Carpet ball
Mineral
　Agate
　Limestone
　Other Mineral
Other Material
　Wood
　Steel
　Paper-mache

Machine-Made Marbles (categorized by manufacturer or design)
Manufacturer
　Transitional
　M.F. Christensen & Son Company
　Akro Agate Company
　Christensen Agate Company
　Peltier Glass Company
　Master Marble/Master Glass Company
　Vitro Agate Company
　Marble King, Incorporated
　Ravenswood Novelty Company
　The Alley companies
　Heaton Agate Company
　Cairo Novelty Company
　Champion Agate, Incorporated
　Davis Marble Works
　Jackson Marble Company
　C.E. Bogard, Company
　JABO, Inc.
　Jabo-Vitro Agate Company
　Other American manufacturers
　Vacor de Mexico
　German manufacturers.
　Other foreign manufacturers

Design
>   Single-stream
>   Single-color
>   Slag
>   Swirl
>   Variegated-stream or Multiple-stream
>   Swirl
>   Corkscrew
>   Patch
>   Ribbon
>   Cat's-eye
>   Brushed
>   Veneered

Contemporary Handmade
>   Hot Glass
>   Torchwork

There are some marble types that are rarer than others. Rarer means that there are less of them available, implying that less of them were produced. This can be due to any one or combination of factors. For instance, certain glass colors are more expensive than others to produce. Or, certain types of marbles involve greater technical skill than others to produce, and were produced in lesser quantities. Rarity is not necessarily an indicator of price. A marble can be so rare that it is unrecognized by most collectors, and have a low price because of low demand. The hobby of marble collecting has also not reached maturity. As a result, the price structure at the high end of the market is quite compressed. The relation between rarity and price is not linear. This means that just because one particular marble is 100 times rarer than another particular type, it is not going to sell for 100 times more. The multiple will tend to be much less.

The second factor that determines the value of a marble is its condition. The grading of condition is very subjective. Every collector has their own opinion and no two collectors will ever agree on the exact condition of a particular marble. Collectors use interchangeably a descriptive grading system (Mint, Near Mint, Good, Collectible), and a numerical grading system based on a scale of 1 to 10. The descriptions of each grading label along with the equivalent numerical grading is:

Mint: A marble that is in original condition. The surface is unmarked and undamaged. There may be some minor rubbing on the surface; however, the marble is just the way it came from the factory. (10.0-9.0)

Near Mint: A marble that has seen minor usage. There may be evidence of some hit marks, usually tiny subsurface moons, pinprick chips, tiny flakes or tiny bruises. The damage is inconsequential and does not detract from viewing the marble. If there is noticeable damage, then it is on only one side of the marble and the other side is Mint. (8.9-8.0)

Good: A marble that has seen usage. It will have numerous hit marks, subsurface moons, chips, flakes or bruises. The core can still be seen clearly, but the marble has obviously been used. If the damage is large or deep, then it is confined to one side and the other side is Mint to Near Mint. (7.9-7.0).

Collectible: A marble that has seen significant usage, with overall moons, chips, flakes, and bruises. The core is completely obscured in some spots. A Collectible marble has served its purpose and been well used. Still, it is a placeholder in a collection until a better example comes along. (6.9-0.0).

Any damage to the surface of a marble, no matter how slight, will affect its value. For a given amount of damage, the depreciation of value is much greater for machine-made marbles than for handmade marbles. Even a small chip will effectively reduce the value of a machine-made marble by more than half. Collectors tend to be more forgiving of damage to a handmade marble, probably because handmade marbles are more difficult to find.

The third factor that determines the value of a marble is its size. The size of a marble is measured by its diameter in inches. Marble manufacturers utilized a sieve system of measuring. Using a device that measured marbles in 1/16" increments, the smallest opening that the marble would fall through was the size. Because of this method, the marbles classified as one size by a manufacturer, could in fact vary by 3/64". It was technically impossible to produce a handmade glass marble in sizes much greater than about 2-3/4" in diameter. The marble would sag and deform during the annealing process because of its weight. However, different types of marbles are more common in some sizes than others. Machine-made marbles are usually 1/2" to 3/4". This is because marble tournament regulations set the size of the shooters to be between 1/2" and 3/4" and the size of the target marbles to be 5/8". Again, the relative rarity of different sizes varies greatly from one type of marble to the next. This guide shows the approximate value by size for each type of marble. You can use this to infer the relative rarity of different marble sizes by marble type.

The final factor that determines the value of a marble is its eye appeal. Eye appeal is related to the brightness of the colors and the symmetry of the design. Brightly colored marbles command higher prices. Also, symmetrical or intricate designs tend to command higher prices. Keep in mind that eye appeal is very subjective, more so than condition. Thus, two collectors could value the same marble very differently.

There are no hard and fast rules for determining the value of a marble. You must take each of these four factors into consideration when valuing a marble and bear in mind that the value you decide may be far different from the value that the next collector comes up with.

HANDMADE MARBLES

A handmade marble is a thing of beauty and a technical feat of glasswork and art. While these marbles were made using the "mass production" techniques of the time, in reality each handmade marble is individually crafted by a person. This cannot be said for machine-made marbles. Each handmade marble carries with it the individual stamp of the craftsman who created it. This is in the twist of the marble and in the design and the colors. The appeal of handmade marbles lies in their individuality. No two canes were the same, and no two marbles off the same rod are exactly the same. You cannot say that about most machine-made marbles.

By definition, a handmade marble is a marble that was individually made by a craftsman. Non-glass handmade marbles have existed for almost as long as there have been children. During primitive and medieval times, these were rounded stone or clay marbles and command a high price today. They lack eye appeal and come in a very limited number of colors and styles, so the supply far outstrips demand. The handmade marbles sought after by today's collectors are those that were produced in Germany during the second half of the nineteenth century and the first two decades of the twentieth century. (Some handmade marbles were produced in the United States during the early twentieth century, but these represented a very tiny segment of the market compared to German marbles. It has also been reported that some handmade marbles were produced in England, although scant evidence has emerged to support this contention).

German-made glass marbles represented the bulk of the marble market until the 1920s. The supremacy of German marbles on the playing field finally ended during the early 1900s due to a combination of several factors. These factors include the American invention of mechanized marble production, the cut-off of German imports into the U.S. during World War I, and the Fordney-McCumber Act tariffs of the early 1920s.

All handmade glass marbles have at least one pontil. This is the rough spot at the bottom pole of the marble where it was sheared off its glass cane or a punty.

Handmade marbles are generally classified as either cane-cut (sometimes called rod-cut) or as single-gather. Almost all handmade glass marbles are cane-cut marbles. This type of marble starts as a cane of glass that contains the design of the marble. The end of the cane is rounded, and then the partially completed sphere is sheared off the end of the cane and then is rounded. Single-gather marbles, on the other hand, are produced one at a time on the end of a punty. Handmade marbles can be further classified by the type and/or coloring of the design.

The production of handmade marbles (whether cane-cut or single-gather) was very labor-intensive. For example, the creation of a handmade swirl required between four and twelve separate manual steps. Single-gather marbles could require less steps, but only one marble was produced at a time, rather than a whole set of marbles off of one cane. The production of handmade marbles was a fairly laborious task. As a result, far fewer handmade marbles exist than machine-made marbles, thereby increasing their value.

The earliest articles discussing marbles appeared in the 1940s. In the mid-1960s articles began describing marbles as collectibles. These articles all dealt with handmade marbles. Early marble collectors, and the hobby is really only about thirty-five years old, were only interested in handmade marbles. The earliest guide to marble collecting was Morrison and Terrison's *Marbles-Identification and Price Guide*, published in 1968, followed by Baumann's *Collecting Antique Marbles*, published in 1970. Both of these books classified handmade marbles, to almost the complete exclusion of machine-made marbles.

The past decade has seen the handmade segment of the marble market begin to mature. This side of the market has not been experiencing the volatility in price that we have seen in the machine-made side of the market. This does not mean that handmades do not go through price cycles. Different types of handmade marbles go in and out of favor with collectors as their tastes change, but the market has been much less volatile than the machine-made market. Recently, there has been an explosion of interest in modern handmade marbles. Fifteen years ago there were only a handful of artists and craftsmen making glass and china spheres. And there were only a few serious collectors. The number of makers and collectors has increased by orders of magnitude during the past five year.

LATTICINIO CORE SWIRLS

Latticinio core swirls are cane-cut marbles. The core consists of strands of colored rods that form a lattice-looking core when the marble is twisted off the cane.

White cores are the most common, occurring in about 80% of the examples. Yellow cores occur in about 10% of the examples. Orange cores and green cores are rare, occurring in about 2% of the examples. Red cores or blue cores are the most rare, occurring in very few examples. Alternating strands of two or more different colors are also rare, with white and yellow alternating being the least difficult to locate.

Outer layers usually consist of sets of strands or bands. Three-layer and four- or five-layer examples are also rare. There are very few examples known to exist with completely formed latticinio cores and no outer layer (naked core). These are very difficult to assign a value to. Left-hand twist examples are also very rare. Some latticinio core swirls have also been found with some mica flecks in them, but these have been very rare. Usually it seems that some stray pieces of mica were laying on the table and picked up when the cane was rolled, however there are some very rare examples where the mica appears to be intentionally part of the design.

When a marble cane is made, the larger cane is cut into sections approximately two feet long. These more manageable canes are then used to produce the marbles. Since swirls are cut off the end of a cane, there are first-off-cane and last-off-cane examples. A first-off-cane swirl comes from the very end of the larger cane. It either has the inner design coming right out of the top of the marble or the design is only partially present at the top. Last-off-cane swirls have the inner design going only partly into the marble, from the top. The bottom of the marble is usually clear or cloudy glass. This is because the last-off-cane swirl was the nub of the cane that was left over. It was usually attached to a punty with clear glass, resulting in part of the marble not having a design. First-off-cane and last-off-cane marbles are generally valued higher than a similar "middle" cane example.

You may also find latticinio core swirls that have a base glass that is a color other than clear. Usually, these are tinted green or blue. Tinted glass is unusual, but not necessarily rare. Swirls with true colored glass, typically amber, blue or green, are much more rare.

#1. Swirl, Latticinio
Core. 1-5/8". $150.

#2. Swirl, Latticinio
Core. 1-1/4". $75.

Latticinio Core Swirls

Up to:		9.9-9.7	9.6-9.3	9.2-9.0	8.9-8.5	8.4-8.0	7.9-7.0
1/2"	High	25.00	14.00	25.45	10.49	2.00	NA
	Low	4.00	6.00	3.00	0.75	2.00	NA
	Average	9.36	8.75	8.06	4.71	2.00	NA
	Quantity	62	4	26	10	2	0
5/8"	High	42.00	34.00	20.50	11.00	9.00	10.00
	Low	11.59	4.00	3.00	1.00	1.00	1.00
	Average	12.40	10.90	6.99	4.85	3.78	3.75
	Quantity	118	25	57	41	8	4
3/4"	High	67.00	46.00	31.00	22.00	17.00	12.00
	Low	5.00	4.00	2.00	1.00	0.50	0.25
	Average	17.72	15.64	11.79	6.69	5.85	7.01
	Quantity	82	31	191	73	18	15
7/8"	High	210.00	180.00	110.00	79.00	17.53	16.00
	Low	15.00	11.00	4.00	3.00	5.00	6.00
	Average	38.23	28.78	21.92	12.94	9.43	11.67
	Quantity	17	8	40	24	8	3
1"	High	274.00	251.00	275.00	100.00	24.00	45.00
	Low	25.00	20.00	15.00	3.00	9.00	5.00
	Average	42.71	36.88	35.71	19.27	12.97	12.24
	Quantity	7	8	14	22	3	9
1-1/4"	High	525.00	400.00	320.00	100.00	70.00	65.00
	Low	27.00	42.00	23.00	17.00	16.00	8.00
	Average	123.54	74.50	58.77	44.79	29.83	26.15
	Quantity	18	4	20	21	6	10
1-1/2"	High	230.00	300.00	150.00	150.00	80.00	72.00
	Low	140.00	47.00	70.00	50.00	50.00	9.00
	Average	170.00	149.50	120.00	106.25	65.00	30.50
	Quantity	3	6	9	4	2	12
1-3/4"	High	550.00	195.00	240.00	250.00	127.50	50.00
	Low	110.00	195.00	120.00	55.00	53.00	15.00
	Average	305.00	195.00	180.00	112.81	56.50	37.14
	Quantity	4	1	2	16	7	7
2"	High	365.00	NA	485.00	310.00	130.00	135.00
	Low	365.00	NA	115.00	130.00	125.00	45.00
	Average	365.00	NA	275.94	185.00	127.50	76.67
	Quantity	1	0	16	4	2	3
2-1/4"	High	NA	NA	750.00	250.00	140.00	175.00
	Low	NA	NA	210.00	140.00	140.00	33.00
	Average	NA	NA	431.11	199.17	140.00	114.87
	Quantity	0	0	9	6	1	16
2-1/2"	High	NA	NA	NA	290.00	205.00	200.00
	Low	NA	NA	NA	210.00	190.00	190.00
	Average	NA	NA	NA	240.00	197.50	180.00
	Quantity	0	0	0	3	2	2

DIVIDED OR
OPEN CORE SWIRLS

The core of a divided core swirl is formed by three or more separate bands. When the marble is twisted off the cane, the bands form a core with clear spaces in between each band.

The determinants of value of a divided core swirl are the number of inner bands, coloring, quality of workmanship, and design. Cores with three or four bands are the most common. Five-banded cores are rarer. Six-banded cores are much rarer. The more closely that the outer bands or strands mirror the spaces in the core, the better designed is the marble.

Three-layer and four-layer examples are rare. Some examples have been found with green aventurine in the inner or outer bands. This is also rare. There are also some rare "naked" examples with no outer layer.

#3. Swirl, Divided Core. 3/4". $35.

#4. Swirl, Divided Core. 1". $40.

Divided Core Swirls

Up to:		9.9-9.7	9.6-9.3	9.2-9.0	8.9-8.5	8.4-8.0	7.9-7.0
1/2"	High	20.00	25.00	16.49	12.00	2.00	NA
	Low	4.00	6.00	3.00	1.00	2.00	NA
	Average	8.96	8.77	7.51	7.96	2.00	NA
	Quantity	36	7	15	11	1	0
5/8"	High	35.00	15.08	29.00	17.50	NA	17.00
	Low	5.00	4.00	2.00	1.00	NA	1.00
	Average	12.61	7.39	7.52	5.87	NA	5.32
	Quantity	65	18	58	26	NA	5
3/4"	High	50.00	120.00	91.00	23.00	14.05	17.00
	Low	6.00	7.00	3.00	1.00	2.00	0.25
	Average	16.58	13.13	11.92	6.49	6.76	5.51
	Quantity	55	26	63	63	8	7
7/8"	High	65.00	50.00	125.00	32.00	12.00	11.00
	Low	12.00	15.00	6.00	5.00	7.00	1.00
	Average	31.69	22.57	17.88	12.09	9.75	6.05
	Quantity	16	7	42	22	4	5
1"	High	150.00	40.00	180.00	50.00	75.00	12.00
	Low	27.00	22.00	17.00	8.00	4.00	4.99

	Average	47.00	28.10	26.47	20.73	18.50	6.81
	Quantity	11	5	21	11	11	4
1-1/4"	High	380.00	325.00	150.00	80.00	25.00	49.00
	Low	55.00	25.00	24.00	15.00	10.00	8.00
	Average	144.37	129.28	64.00	30.58	18.62	13.80
	Quantity	8	6	6	13	8	10
1-1/2"	High	300.00	150.00	150.00	210.00	90.00	53.00
	Low	125.00	150.00	103.00	11.00	30.00	8.00
	Average	190.43	150.00	122.60	86.38	46.53	31.12
	Quantity	7	1	5	10	13	16
1-3/4"	High	NA	220.00	260.00	130.00	150.00	66.00
	Low	NA	220.00	110.00	45.00	40.00	17.00
	Average	NA	220.00	166.67	115.90	94.37	35.32
	Quantity	0	1	6	14	13	14
2"	High	NA	320.00	NA	147.50	90.00	100.00
	Low	NA	300.00	NA	110.00	34.00	28.00
	Average	NA	310.00	NA	128.75	60.67	50.53
	Quantity	0	2	0	2	6	15
2-1/4"	High	410.00	400.00	350.00	231.00	240.00	NA
	Low	410.00	272.00	305.00	231.00	170.00	NA
	Average	410.00	336.00	327.50	231.00	205.00	NA
	Quantity	1	2	2	1	2	0
2-1/2"	High	NA	NA	NA	NA	290.00	75.00
	Low	NA	NA	NA	NA	290.00	56.88
	Average	NA	NA	NA	NA	290.00	65.94
	Quantity	0	0	0	0	1	2

SOLID CORE SWIRLS

The core of a solid core swirl is formed by bands or strands of color that are placed so closely together that there are no clear spaces in the core in between. The core can be all the same color, usually white or yellow, or it can be a solid color with colored bands or stripes on it.

Solid core swirls usually have an outer layer of bands or strands. "Naked" solid core swirls, marbles without an outer layer, are rare, but are more common than found in latticinio or divided core swirls. Examples with three or four layers are also rare. Occasionally, the core of the swirl will have three or four lobes. Aventurine has been found in the cores or the outer layers of a few examples. This is rare. Also, some very few examples have been found in colored base glass. This is also very rare.

There are some solid core swirls (as well as latticinio core and divided core) that have very bright colors. These tend to command a price premium.

#5. Swirl, Solid Core. 3/4". $35.

#6. Swirl, Solid Core. 1-3/8". $150.

Solid Core Swirls

Up to:		9.9-9.7	9.6-9.3	9.2-9.0	8.9-8.5	8.4-8.0	7.9-7.0
1/2"	High	20.00	25.00	16.49	12.00	2.00	NA
	Low	4.00	6.00	3.00	1.00	2.00	NA
	Average	8.96	8.77	7.51	7.96	2.00	NA
	Quantity	36	7	15	11	1	0
5/8"	High	35.00	15.08	29.00	17.50	NA	17.00
	Low	5.00	4.00	2.00	1.00	NA	1.00
	Average	12.61	7.39	7.52	5.87	NA	5.32
	Quantity	65	18	58	26	NA	5
3/4"	High	50.00	120.00	91.00	23.00	14.05	17.00
	Low	6.00	7.00	3.00	1.00	2.00	0.25
	Average	16.58	13.13	11.92	6.49	6.76	5.51
	Quantity	55	26	63	63	8	7
7/8"	High	65.00	50.00	125.00	32.00	12.00	11.00
	Low	12.00	15.00	6.00	5.00	7.00	1.00
	Average	31.69	22.57	17.88	12.09	9.75	6.05
	Quantity	16	7.00	42	22	4	5
1"	High	150.00	40.00	180.00	50.00	75.00	12.00
	Low	27.00	22.00	17.00	8.00	4.00	4.99
	Average	47.00	28.10	26.47	20.73	18.50	6.81
	Quantity	11	5	21	11	11	4
1-1/4"	High	380.00	325.00	150.00	80.00	25.00	49.00
	Low	55.00	25.00	24.00	15.00	10.00	8.00
	Average	144.37	129.28	64.00	30.58	18.62	13.80
	Quantity	8	6	6	13	8	10
1-1/2"	High	300.00	150.00	150.00	210.00	90.00	53.00
	Low	125.00	150.00	103.00	11.00	30.00	8.00
	Average	190.43	150.00	122.60	86.38	46.53	31.12
	Quantity	7	1	5	10	13	16
1-3/4"	High	NA	220.00	260.00	130.00	150.00	66.00
	Low	NA	220.00	110.00	45.00	40.00	17.00
	Average	NA	220.00	166.67	115.90	94.37	35.32
	Quantity	0	1	6	14	13	14
2"	High	NA	320.00	NA	147.50	90.00	100.00
	Low	NA	300.00	NA	110.00	34.00	28.00
	Average	NA	310.00	NA	128.75	60.67	50.53
	Quantity	0	2	0	2	6	15
2-1/4"	High	410.00	400.00	350.00	231.00	240.00	NA
	Low	410.00	272.00	305.00	231.00	170.00	NA
	Average	410.00	336.00	327.50	231.00	205.00	NA
	Quantity	1	2	2	1	2	0
2-1/2"	High	NA	NA	NA	NA	290.00	75.00
	Low	NA	NA	NA	NA	290.00	56.88
	Average	NA	NA	NA	NA	290.00	65.94
	Quantity	0	0	0	0	1	2

RIBBON
CORE SWIRLS

The core of a ribbon core swirl is a wide, flat band of color in the center of a rod. This band is twisted when the marble is cut off the cane. The degree of twist will vary from perfectly flat (no twist) to three or four twists (creating a helix effect).

The core of a ribbon core swirl is usually a solid color with several strands or bands of color on it. It will vary in thickness. The core can consist of one ribbon, which is called a single ribbon, or two ribbons, which is called a double ribbon. Double ribbon core swirls are slightly more common than single ribbon cores.

Ribbon core swirls can either be naked or have outer bands or strands. Naked core ribbon swirls are slightly rarer than those with outer layers. The outer layer of a ribbon core swirl usually mirrors the face of the ribbon, as opposed to the edge. The better designed and executed the outer layer and ribbon, the more valuable the marble.

#7. Swirl, Ribbon Core. 7/8". $100.   #8. Swirl, Ribbon Core. 23/32". $50.

Ribbon Core Swirls

Up to:		9.9-9.7	9.6-9.3	9.2-9.0	8.9-8.5	8.4-8.0	7.9-7.0
1/2"	High	42.00	25.00	NA	NA	NA	NA
	Low	13.00	25.00	NA	NA	NA	NA
	Average	25.33	25.00	NA	NA	NA	NA
	Quantity	3	1	0	0	0	0
5/8"	High	110.00	32.00	75.00	33.00	20.00	11.00
	Low	26.00	17.00	3.00	2.00	3.00	11.00
	Average	41.30	29.50	28.08	19.00	12.39	11.00
	Quantity	15	8	12	5	NA	1
3/4"	High	360.00	50.00	110.00	70.00	33.00	17.00
	Low	29.00	31.00	15.00	8.00	7.00	5.00
	Average	75.43	45.50	41.96	19.57	14.85	10.22
	Quantity	21	25	15	28	7	9
7/8"	High	675.00	1150.00	650.00	245.00	130.00	27.00
	Low	125.00	150.00	27.00	7.00	10.00	6.00
	Average	179.40	168.42	67.42	56.11	25.20	15.25
	Quantity	5	5	31	41	28	4

1"	High	NA	190.00	150.00	175.00	NA	14.00
	Low	NA	190.00	35.00	19.00	NA	8.00
	Average	NA	190.00	76.25	70.91	NA	11.42
	Quantity	0	1	4	12 `	0	7
1-1/4"	High	230.00	200.00	300.00	210.37	75.00	22.00
	Low	170.00	80.00	110.00	85.00	17.00	22.00
	Average	209.99	160.00	156.67	107.59	45.77	22.00
	Quantity	5	8	3	5	9	1
1-1/2"	High	NA	600.00	175.00	NA	65.00	50.00
	Low	NA	235.00	175.00	NA	60.00	50.00
	Average	NA	247.50	175.00	NA	62.50	50.00
	Quantity	0	7	1	0	2	1
1-3/4"	High	NA	NA	425.00	250.00	75.00	NA
	Low	NA	NA	335.00	250.00	75.00	NA
	Average	NA	NA	380.00	250.00	75.00	NA
	Quantity	0	0	2	1	1	0
2"	High	NA	NA	450.00	260.00	NA	NA
	Low	NA	NA	450.00	260.00	NA	NA
	Average	NA	NA	450.00	260.00	NA	NA
	Quantity	0	0	1	1	0	0

JOSEPH'S COAT SWIRLS

Joseph's Coat swirls are swirls that have an outer layer of glass that is composed of variously colored similar-width complete strands, packed very closely together.

Better examples have no clear spaces in between the strands. Some examples do have clear spaces. In some cases, these appear to be part of the design. There are usually some strands in the inner core that can be seen through the spaces. Generally, the more colors in the marble, the more valuable it is.

Joseph's Coat swirls have either dark, earthy colors or bright colors. The base glass of a Joseph's Coat can either be clear or colored.

#9. Swirl, Joseph Coat.
1-1/4". $250.

#10. Swirl, Joseph Coat.
1". $250.

Joseph's Coat Swirls

Up to:		9.9-9.7	9.6-9.3	9.2-9.0	8.9-8.5	8.4-8.0	7.9-7.0
1/2"	High	42.00	NA	NA	NA	NA	NA
	Low	42.00	NA	NA	NA	NA	NA
	Average	42.00	NA	NA	NA	NA	NA
	Quantity	1	0	0	0	0	0
5/8"	High	120.00	80.00	72.50	30.00	NA	NA
	Low	29.20	40.00	15.00	19.00	NA	NA
	Average	70.65	55.33	31.92	24.50	NA	NA
	Quantity	11	3	19	6	0	0
3/4"	High	210.00	80.00	50.00	34.00	23.00	NA
	Low	55.00	55.00	22.00	15.00	6.00	NA
	Average	111.25	66.25	33.33	25.00	14.75	NA
	Quantity	4	4	9	5	4	0
7/8"	High	223.00	260.00	130.00	110.00	32.00	NA
	Low	223.00	80.00	50.00	17.00	32.00	NA
	Average	223.00	179.83	89.33	65.00	32.00	NA
	Quantity	1	8	3	5	1	0
1"	High	525.00	480.00	370.00	320.00	NA	110.00
	Low	110.00	91.00	80.00	90.00	NA	51.00
	Average	354.00	290.20	209.17	191.39	NA	80.50
	Quantity	5	5	15	9	0	2
1-1/4"	High	230.00	200.00	300.00	210.37	75.00	22.00
	Low	170.00	80.00	110.00	85.00	17.00	22.00
	Average	209.99	160.00	156.67	107.59	45.77	22.00
	Quantity	5	8	3	5	9	1
1-1/2"	High	NA	600.00	175.00	NA	65.00	50.00
	Low	NA	235.00	175.00	NA	60.00	50.00
	Average	NA	247.50	175.00	NA	62.50	50.00
	Quantity	0	7	1	0	2	1
1-3/4"	High	NA	NA	425.00	250.00	75.00	NA
	Low	NA	NA	335.00	250.00	75.00	NA
	Average	NA	NA	380.00	250.00	75.00	NA
	Quantity	0	0	2	1	1	0

BANDED OR CORELESS SWIRLS

The category banded swirls and coreless swirls tends to be used interchangeably. These are swirls that have an outer layer of bands or strands, but no inner core. If the outer layer appears to be evenly spaced, subsurface, and of a type usually found as the outer layer of other types of swirls, then they are usually termed coreless. If the outer layer is on the surface, irregular in spacing and band width, and not the type of outer layer typically seen on a swirl, then they are termed banded. They tend to lack the pizzazz of other types of swirls and are valued lower. Coreless swirls, as opposed to banded swirls, tend to carry somewhat more value.

Banded and coreless swirls are found with colored base glass (usually blue or green), about as often as they are found in clear. There is not much difference in value between the different colors.

Joseph's Coat swirls are a specialized variety of banded swirls. If the bands are very thin and packed closely together, then it is a Joseph's Coat swirl. Otherwise, it is a banded swirl.

#11. Swirl, Banded/Coreless. 21/32". $15.

#12. Swirl, Banded/Coreless. 11/16". $20.

Banded or Coreless Swirls

Up to:		9.9-9.7	9.6-9.3	9.2-9.0	8.9-8.5	8.4-8.0	7.9-7.0
1/2"	High	15.00	5.00	NA	5.00	NA	NA
	Low	4.00	5.00	NA	1.00	NA	NA
	Average	7.08	5.00	NA	2.66	NA	NA
	Quantity	10	1	0	3	0	0
5/8"	High	30.00	15.00	15.00	16.02	3.25	NA
	Low	4.00	4.00	3.00	3.00	3.25	NA
	Average	11.17	9.20	8.23	7.38	3.25	NA
	Quantity	28	12	17	6	1	0
3/4"	High	30.00	30.00	31.00	17.00	25.00	18.00
	Low	6.00	5.00	3.00	2.00	2.00	1.00
	Average	14.25	12.88	12.84	6.90	10.80	9.00
	Quantity	56	18	23	19	6	9
7/8"	High	23.00	17.00	19.00	17.00	NA	15.00
	Low	14.00	12.00	19.00	4.00	NA	0.50
	Average	18.50	14.74	19.00	9.12	NA	7.50
	Quantity	2	4	1	10	0	3

PEPPERMINT SWIRLS

A peppermint swirl is another specific type of banded swirl that has subsurface bands. The marble has two wide opaque white bands, alternating with two thinner translucent blue bands. There are usually three or two transparent pink stripes on each white band.

Less common are marbles with a single transparent pink stripe on each white band. Some marbles exist that have two pink bands, which are the same width as the two blue bands. These are called "beach ball" and are much rarer than the other types. There have also been a few marbles found with an odd number of pink bands (three or five). These are extremely rare.

Marbles with mica in the blue bands are very rare. There have also been some marbles found with a blue strand in one of the pink strands or with a green strand in the blue band. These are also very rare, but do not seem to have any higher value.

#13. Swirl, Peppermint.
21/32". $65.

#14. Swirl, Peppermint with mica.
21/32". $300.

Peppermint Swirls

Up to:		9.9-9.7	9.6-9.3	9.2-9.0	8.9-8.5	8.4-8.0	7.9-7.0
5/8"	High	125.00	90.00	56.00	37.00	38.00	NA
	Low	42.00	39.00	36.00	32.00	15.00	NA
	Average	67.00	51.00	42.00	34.50	29.33	NA
	Quantity	12	8	6	2	3	0
3/4"	High	NA	NA	90.00	76.00	37.00	24.00
	Low	NA	NA	37.00	20.49	25.00	24.00
	Average	NA	NA	68.00	42.41	32.67	24.00
	Quantity	0	0	4	7	3	1
7/8"	High	NA	NA	NA	90.00	41.00	37.00
	Low	NA	NA	NA	32.00	12.00	11.00
	Average	NA	NA	NA	53.00	33.83	25.40
	Quantity	0	0	0	3	12	5

#15. Swirl, Custard.
11/16". $75.

#16. Swirl, Cornhusk.
3/4". $75.

#17. Swirl, Caramel.
11/16". $100.

#18. Swirl, Butterscotch.
11/16". $60.

#19. Swirl, Gooseberry.
11/16". $75.

CLAMBROTHS

#20. Clambroth.
11/16". $200.

A clambroth is a swirl that has an opaque base with colored strands on the surface. The strands are generally equidistantly spaced.

The base color is usually opaque white. Some opalescent bases have been found. The most common colors for strands are pink, blue or green. A clambroth that has strands of more than one color, usually alternating, is called "multicolored". These are rarer than the single-color marbles. Marbles with a base glass color that is not white, usually black or blue, are also rare.

There are two different types of glass that were used for the base glass. One type is relatively hard, like other glass marbles, and does not chip easily. The other type is very soft and bruises quite easily. Some collectors believe that the hard type is German, while the soft type is early American. This does not appear to affect the value of the marble.

Missing strands or poor spacing of the strands results in a discount. Clambroths usually have eight to eighteen strands (depending on the marble size). There are some clambroths that have thirty or more strands. These are called "cased" clambroths and are very rare. There are also clambroths that are "cased" in a layer of clear glass. These are also very rare.

#21. Clambroth.
5/8". $350.

Clambroths

Up to:		9.9-9.7	9.6-9.3	9.2-9.0	8.9-8.5	8.4-8.0	7.9-7.0
5/8"	High	120.00	NA	285.00	120.00	90.00	NA
	Low	120.00	NA	47.00	40.50	65.00	NA
	Average	120.00	NA	114.71	79.07	75.00	NA
	Quantity	1	0	7	7	3	0
3/4"	High	350.00	NA	NA	140.00	100.00	150.00
	Low	300.00	NA	NA	15.00	25.00	24.00
	Average	316.66	NA	NA	82.83	44.14	38.69
	Quantity	3	0	0	6	7	8
7/8"	High	NA	525.00	225.00	240.00	100.00	NA
	Low	NA	525.00	225.00	80.00	50.00	NA
	Average	NA	525.00	225.00	143.33	78.00	NA
	Quantity	0	1	1	3	5	0

BANDED OPAQUES

A banded opaque has either an opaque or semi-opaque base glass. The surface of the marble has colored strands, bands or stretched colored flecks on it.

A "swirl-type" banded opaque has colored strands and bands that are unbroken from pole to pole. An "end-of-day-type" banded opaque has bands of stretched colored flecks on the surface. The stretched flecks generally are not continuous from pole to pole. One type does not seem to be any rarer than the other, but the "swirl-type" are valued slightly higher, probably because they tend to look better-designed.

Marbles with multi-color bands are rarer, as are marbles with a color base glass, rather than the white base. There are some marbles that have either a brightly colored base or brightly colored bands. These are sometimes referred to as "electric" and are valued much higher than other banded opaques.

All else being equal, the greater the surface area that is covered by color, the more valuable the marble.

#22. Banded Opaque.
11/16". $100.

#23. Banded Opaque.
21/32". $200.

Banded Opaques

Up to:		9.9-9.7	9.6-9.3	9.2-9.0	8.9-8.5	8.4-8.0	7.9-7.0
5/8"	High	95.00	70.00	120.00	NA	NA	NA
	Low	32.00	32.00	55.00	NA	NA	NA
	Average	52.06	49.50	95.00	NA	NA	NA
	Quantity	16	16	3	0	0	0
3/4"	High	100.00	NA	125.00	120.00	9.00	42.00
	Low	42.00	NA	32.00	18.00	9.00	10.00
	Average	71.00	NA	65.57	58.50	9.00	18.20
	Quantity	2	0	7	14	2	10
7/8"	High	NA	NA	NA	65.00	42.00	NA
	Low	NA	NA	NA	65.00	25.00	NA
	Average	NA	NA	NA	65.00	31.22	NA
	Quantity	0	0	0	1	3	0

INDIAN

An indian is a marble that has an opaque black base. On the surface are bands consisting of colored strands or stretched colored flecks.

A "swirl-type" indian has colored strands that run unbroken from pole to pole. Usually there is a colored band that consists of subsurface opaque white strands covered by a transparent color. An "end-of-day-type" indian has bands of stretched colored flecks that do not run continuously from pole to pole. "Swirl-type" indians are about as common as "end-of-day type" indians, but are valued more highly, probably because they seem to be better designed.

The surface usually has two bands on it. Multi-band examples are rarer and command a premium. Generally, the more surface area that is covered by color, the more valuable the marble.

There are marbles with a translucent dark red or dark amethyst base glass. These are called "mag-lites" and carry a premium. Blue, green or amber translucents are much rarer.

#24. Indian. 11/16". $60.   #25. Indian. 11/16". $60.

Indians

Up to:		9.9-9.7	9.6-9.3	9.2-9.0	8.9-8.5	8.4-8.0	7.9-7.0
5/8"	High	100.00	90.00	110.00	40.00	12.00	NA
	Low	17.00	15.00	12.00	3.00	10.00	NA
	Average	40.67	37.21	34.14	17.88	11.27	NA
	Quantity	26	28	28	17	4	0
3/4"	High	95.00	90.00	75.00	110.00	30.00	17.00
	Low	25.00	27.00	13.00	13.00	12.00	5.00
	Average	54.62	47.75	39.02	38.89	19.20	10.00
	Quantity	16	8	30	9	5	3
7/8"	High	NA	310.00	50.00	55.00	42.00	17.00
	Low	NA	80.00	45.00	36.00	27.00	12.00
	Average	NA	178.75	47.50	45.50	34.50	14.75
	Quantity	0	7	2	2	2	4
1"	High	NA	NA	310.00	NA	75.00	60.00
	Low	NA	NA	310.00	NA	55.00	13.00
	Average	NA	NA	310.00	NA	65.00	28.83
	Quantity	0	0	1	0	4	6

BANDED LUTZ

A banded lutz is a marble with a single-colored base glass and two sets of two bands alternating with two lutz bands. Lutz is finely ground copper flakes or goldstone. The lutz bands are usually edged by opaque white strands.

The most common base glass is transparent clear. Transparent color base glass is rarer. Semi-opaque base glass (usually colored) is very rare. Opaque base glass is also rare. Marbles with opaque black bases are the most common of this type. Other colors are rarer.

A few rare examples have only two colored bands, rather than the usual four, or extra colored bands. These are extremely rare.

#26. Lutz, Banded. 3/4".
$100.

#27. Lutz, Banded. 21/32".
$500.

#28. Lutz, Banded. 11/16".
$400.

Banded Lutz

Up to:		9.9-9.7	9.6-9.3	9.2-9.0	8.9-8.5	8.4-8.0	7.9-7.0
5/8"	High	505.00	250.00	225.00	180.00	33.00	NA
	Low	95.00	85.00	80.00	65.00	33.00	NA
	Average	154.61	124.48	115.28	96.57	33.00	NA
	Quantity	18	5	39	7	1	0
3/4"	High	350.00	525.00	300.00	200.00	250.00	110.00
	Low	180.00	140.00	110.00	34.00	47.00	35.00
	Average	220.20	208.44	144.66	116.00	79.33	66.00
	Quantity	5	8	15	9	9	3
7/8"	High	NA	NA	NA	NA	NA	NA
	Low	NA	NA	NA	NA	NA	NA
	Average	NA	NA	NA	NA	NA	NA
	Quantity	0	0	0	0	0	0
1"	High	560.00	460.00	320.00	575.00	150.00	47.00
	Low	305.00	190.00	120.00	85.00	40.00	20.00
	Average	332.50	303.33	238.00	183.00	71.09	71.00
	Quantity	5	6	5	6	10	6

ONIONSKIN LUTZ

An onionskin lutz is a marble that has an end of day onionskin core with lutz bands and/or lutz sprinkled on the core.

The base color of the core is usually white, with blue, green or red streaks. Usually the streaks are not as pronounced as they are on an end of day that does not have lutz.

The lutz can vary from a light sprinkling on the core to very heavy lutz bands. Heavy lutz on the core increases the value of the marble. In some instances, the lutz floats on a layer of clear glass above the core. These are rare and are sometimes called "floaters."

A couple of lobed and/or cloud examples are known to exist. These are very rare. Marbles that have colored glass surrounding the core and lutz are also very rare. They are very difficult to value because of their rarity.

#29. Lutz, Onionskin.
5/8". $175.

#30. Lutz, Onionskin.
3/4". $300.

Onionskin Lutz

Up to:			9.9-9.7	9.6-9.3	9.2-9.0	8.9-8.5	8.4-8.0	7.9-7.0
5/8"	High		135.00	NA	1500.00	66.00	NA	38.00
	Low		130.00	NA	85.00	40.00	NA	38.00
	Average		132.50	NA	118.89	53.00	NA	38.00
	Quantity		2	0	9	2	0	1
3/4"	High		NA	NA	150.00	200.00	155.00	50.00
	Low		NA	NA	80.00	30.00	27.00	42.00
	Average		NA	NA	124.17	67.89	49.67	48.00
	Quantity		0	0	6	35	6	4
7/8"	High		NA	NA	NA	NA	NA	NA
	Low		NA	NA	NA	NA	NA	NA
	Average		NA	NA	NA	NA	NA	NA
	Quantity		0	0	0	0	0	0
1"	High		1450.00	NA	300.00	300.00	95.00	70.00
	Low		920.00	NA	250.00	140.00	60.00	70.00
	Average		1035.00	NA	266.66	215.00	78.75	70.00
	Quantity		4	0	3	13	4	1

RIBBON LUTZ

A ribbon lutz is a naked ribbon core swirl with lutz on both edges of the ribbon. There are single ribbon examples and double ribbon examples. No examples are known to exist that have an outer layer of strands or bands.

The basic type is transparent clear base with an opaque white single ribbon core. The ribbon usually has transparent color glass over it. There are some marbles with an opaque-color single ribbon. These are somewhat rarer.

There are examples with a double ribbon, where each ribbon is a different color. These are also rare.

Some marbles are in transparent color glass. The ribbon is always opaque white. These are also rare.

#31. Lutz, Ribbon. 15/16". $700.

#32. Lutz, Ribbon. 5/8". $300.

Ribbon Lutz

Up to:		9.9-9.7	9.6-9.3	9.2-9.0	8.9-8.5	8.4-8.0	7.9-7.0
5/8"	High	NA	NA	360.00	200.00	190.00	110.00
	Low	NA	NA	170.00	80.00	80.00	110.00
	Average	NA	NA	203.89	146.58	111.87	110.00
	Quantity	0	0	9	19	8	3
3/4"	High	NA	290.00	275.00	260.00	200.00	110.00
	Low	NA	261.00	170.00	80.00	80.00	55.00
	Average	NA	277.00	224.09	189.33	151.34	68.57
	Quantity	0	3	11	15	26	7

INDIAN LUTZ

An indian lutz has an opaque black base with three or four lutz bands on the surface. The bands are edged with colored strands. Several examples have also been found with colored bands and lutz bands on the surface. These do not seem to have any additional value.

#33. Lutz, Indian.
11/16". $800.

Indian Lutz

Up to:		9.9-9.7	9.6-9.3	9.2-9.0	8.9-8.5	8.4-8.0	7.9-7.0
11/16"	High	900.00	NA	NA	NA	NA	NA
	Low	750.00	NA	NA	NA	NA	NA
	Average	816.66	NA	NA	NA	NA	NA
	Quantity	3	0	0	0	0	0
3/4"	High	1450.00	NA	NA	NA	NA	NA
	Low	820.00	NA	NA	NA	NA	NA
	Average	1150.00	NA	NA	NA	NA	NA
	Quantity	2	0	0	0	0	0

MIST LUTZ

A mist lutz is a transparent clear base with a core of a transparent color, usually green. There is a layer of lutz floating in the glass layer above the core.

#34. Lutz, Mist. 11/16". $350.

Mist Lutz

Up to:		9.9-9.7	9.6-9.3	9.2-9.0	8.9-8.5	8.4-8.0	7.9-7.0
1/2"	High	380.00	NA	NA	135.00	NA	NA
	Low	380.00	NA	NA	135.00	NA	NA
	Average	380.00	NA	NA	135.00	NA	NA
	Quantity	1	0	0	1	0	0
5/8"	High	320.00	340.00	250.00	NA	150.00	NA
	Low	150.00	340.00	117.00	NA	150.00	NA
	Average	235.00	340.00	178.85	NA	150.00	NA
	Quantity	2	1	7	0	1	0

SOLID CORE LUTZ

A solid core lutz is a transparent clear base with a core of a opaque color, usually black or green. There is a layer of lutz on the core and then a clear outer layer.

#35. Lutz, Solid Core. 11/16". $300.

Solid Core Lutz

Up to:		9.9-9.7	9.6-9.3	9.2-9.0	8.9-8.5	8.4-8.0	7.9-7.0
5/8"	High	400.00	NA	NA	NA	NA	NA
	Low	200.00	NA	NA	NA	NA	NA
	Average	244.00	NA	NA	NA	NA	NA
	Quantity	5	0	0	0	0	0
3/4"	High	570.00	NA	NA	NA	NA	NA
	Low	320.00	NA	NA	NA	NA	NA
	Average	412.50	NA	NA	NA	NA	NA
	Quantity	4	0	0	0	0	0

END OF DAY CLOUD

An End of Day Cloud has a transparent base glass, usually clear. The marble can have either a colored base core or no base core. On the core are flecks of colored glass that were not stretched when the marble was drawn off the rod. This is different than an End of Day Onionskin, where the flecks of color did stretch.

30

Generally, the more colors, the more valuable the marble. Blue or red flecks on a white or yellow background are the most common. Yellow or green flecks, or a different colored background, are rarer.

Some marbles are left-hand twisted. These are rare, although not as rare as Swirl marbles with a left-hand twist. Marbles with mica are rare, although not as rare as Swirls with mica. Some single-gather single-pontil marbles exist. These are much rarer than cane-cut, although single-pontil clouds seem to be more common than single-pontil onionskins. Lobed marbles are also rare and have been found with three to six lobes, and in this instance are rarer than lobed onionskins.

#36. End of Day, Cloud. 1-1/4". $300.

#37. End of Day, Cloud. 1-3/4". $1000.

End of Day Cloud

Up to:		9.9-9.7	9.6-9.3	9.2-9.0	8.9-8.5	8.4-8.0	7.9-7.0
3/4"	High	150.00	225.00	410.00	135.00	13.00	42.00
	Low	90.00	42.00	71.00	85.00	13.00	10.00
	Average	120.00	115.67	200.33	115.00	13.00	22.42
	Quantity	3	3	3	3	1	3
1"	High	NA	NA	170.00	NA	127.50	33.00
	Low	NA	NA	170.00	NA	27.00	33.00
	Average	NA	NA	170.00	NA	86.13	33.00
	Quantity	0	0	1	0	4	1
1-1/2"	High	NA	NA	NA	436.00	65.00	125.00
	Low	NA	NA	NA	160.00	65.00	55.00
	Average	NA	NA	NA	290.20	65.00	83.19
	Quantity	0	0	0	5	1	4
1-3/4"	High	NA	850.00	NA	625.00	460.00	300.00
	Low	NA	850.00	NA	625.00	300.00	35.00
	Average	NA	850.00	NA	625.00	380.00	148.33
	Quantity	0	1	0	1	2	3
2"	High	NA	NA	NA	1050.00	260.00	150.00
	Low	NA	NA	NA	360.00	260.00	150.00
	Average	NA	NA	NA	612.50	260.00	150.00
	Quantity	0	0	0	4	1	1

END OF DAY ONIONSKIN

An End of Day Onionskin has a transparent base glass, usually clear. The marble can have either a colored core or a transparent clear core. On the core are flecks of colored glass that were stretched when the marble was made.

Generally, the base color is white or yellow, and the flecks are red, blue or green. Other colors are rarer.

Some marbles are left-hand twisted. This is rare, although not as rare as in Swirls. Marbles with mica are also rare, although again not as rare as in Swirls. Single-gather, single pontil marbles are rarer than is seen with clouds. Lobed marbles have been found with three to eighteen lobes. These are also rare. Panelled marbles are fairly common and are discussed later.

#38. End of Day, Onionskin with mica. 7/8". $200.

#39. End of Day, Onionskin. 3/4". $50.

End of Day Onionskin

Up to:		9.9-9.7	9.6-9.3	9.2-9.0	8.9-8.5	8.4-8.0	7.9-7.0
1/2"	High	47.00	25.00	44.50	27.00	14.25	NA
	Low	14.00	25.00	9.00	4.00	14.25	NA
	Average	22.77	25.00	19.95	14.71	14.25	NA
	Quantity	37	1	10	7	1	0
5/8"	High	32.00	121.00	66.00	25.00	NA	15.00
	Low	15.00	15.00	9.00	7.00	NA	15.00
	Average	27.85	27.58	25.52	11.36	NA	15.00
	Quantity	37	12	25	11	0	1
3/4"	High	310.00	70.00	75.00	60.00	22.00	8.00
	Low	17.00	15.00	12.00	5.00	3.00	4.00
	Average	58.27	29.84	32.46	17.53	12.67	6.50
	Quantity	22	9	23	29	10	3
1"	High	285.00	121.00	175.00	75.00	20.00	25.00
	Low	45.00	42.00	27.00	15.00	15.00	21.00
	Average	89.44	76.55	61.27	37.36	17.33	23.00
	Quantity	9	9	12	14	3	2

1-1/4"	High	270.00	NA	260.00	45.00	41.00	60.00
	Low	200.00	NA	105.00	45.00	41.00	20.00
	Average	235.00	NA	195.00	45.00	41.00	46.10
	Quantity	2	0	5	1	1	5
1-1/2"	High	725.00	NA	635.00	370.00	275.00	120.00
	Low	150.00	NA	110.00	120.00	32.00	22.00
	Average	337.50	NA	238.33	195.00	103.20	51.00
	Quantity	4	0	6	6	10	4
1-3/4"	High	NA	NA	NA	725.00	NA	60.00
	Low	NA	NA	NA	95.00	NA	31.00
	Average	NA	NA	NA	338.33	NA	45.50
	Quantity	0	0	0	7	0	2
2"	High	NA	NA	NA	370.00	190.00	140.00
	Low	NA	NA	NA	200.00	125.00	140.00
	Average	NA	NA	NA	303.33	157.50	140.00
	Quantity	0	0	0	6	2	1

END OF DAY PANELLED ONIONSKIN

An End of Day Panelled Cloud or Onionskin is a cloud or onionskin that has two or more distinct groups of colors. The most common have four panels. Two of the panels are stretched red flecks on a white or yellow background, alternating with two panels of green or blue flecks on the background not used in the first panels. Panels of one colored flecks alternating with panels of different colored flecks, but all on the same color background are also fairly common. Other color combinations are rarer. About 90% of the paneled onionskins have four panels. Other numbers of panels are rarer.

Some marbles are left-hand twisted. This is rare, although more common than in swirls. Some marbles have mica, which is rare, and some are single-gather, single-pontil marbles. There are some lobed marbles. These are rare and usually the lobes mirror the panels.

#40. End of Day, Paneled Onionskin. 27/32". $400.

#41. End of Day, Paneled Onionskin. 27/32". $200.

END OF DAY
PANELLED ONIONSKIN

Up to:		9.9-9.7	9.6-9.3	9.2-9.0	8.9-8.5	8.4-8.0	7.9-7.0
1/2"	High	70.00	NA	NA	21.00	12.50	NA
	Low	14.00	NA	NA	8.00	4.00	NA
	Average	29.58	NA	NA	14.50	8.37	NA
	Quantity	19	0	0	2	4	0
5/8"	High	150.00	120.00	80.00	42.00	11.00	12.00
	Low	13.00	12.00	5.00	6.00	11.00	9.00
	Average	30.99	31.30	27.44	16.64	11.00	10.00
	Quantity	44	15	25	21	1	3
3/4"	High	75.00	80.00	110.00	110.00	38.00	20.50
	Low	20.00	19.00	13.00	8.00	15.00	2.00
	Average	35.21	32.16	30.36	28.38	20.75	7.80
	Quantity	14	12	22	28	4	15
7/8"	High	300.00	320.00	225.00	105.00	50.00	60.00
	Low	65.00	42.00	19.00	13.00	15.00	7.00
	Average	178.33	108.29	57.47	47.39	30.58	20.89
	Quantity	9	7	34	24	12	12
1"	High	190.00	300.00	103.00	50.00	46.00	37.00
	Low	120.00	100.00	42.00	17.00	10.00	15.00
	Average	160.00	155.00	81.17	32.60	29.44	25.00
	Quantity	3	6	7	5	9	3
1-1/4"	High	250.00	NA	80.00	65.00	90.00	NA
	Low	250.00	NA	80.00	50.00	25.00	NA
	Average	250.00	NA	80.00	57.50	50.68	NA
	Quantity	1	0	1	2	7	0
1-1/2"	High	NA	NA	310.00	160.00	110.00	24.00
	Low	NA	NA	310.00	70.00	33.00	24.00
	Average	NA	NA	310.00	108.33	80.60	24.00
	Quantity	0	0	1	3	5	1
1-3/4"	High	NA	NA	625.00	310.00	120.00	110.00
	Low	NA	NA	220.00	60.00	46.00	20.00
	Average	NA	NA	335.00	166.56	78.20	54.77
	Quantity	0	0	3	15	5	11
2"	High	450.00	445.00	430.00	375.00	300.00	90.00
	Low	450.00	385.00	110.00	110.00	65.00	55.00
	Average	450.00	415.00	380.00	238.33	182.50	77.50
	Quantity	1	2	9	6	2	4
2-1/4"	High	NA	800.00	NA	430.00	370.00	125.00
	Low	NA	800.00	NA	240.00	300.00	125.00
	Average	NA	800.00	NA	335.00	330.00	125.00
	Quantity	0	1	0	2	4	1
2-1/2"	High	NA	NA	NA	500.00	200.00	150.00
	Low	NA	NA	NA	500.00	200.00	150.00
	Average	NA	NA	NA	500.00	200.00	150.00
	Quantity	0	0	0	1	1	1

END OF DAY SUBMARINE

An End of Day Submarine is sometimes referred to as a Coreless Onionskin. It has a transparent base (usually clear) with subsurface stretched bands of color. The colors are usually bright. They are distinguished from Onionskins as not having a color on a core or subsurface layer. Rather they are constructed without a core or subsurface color.

#42. End of Day, Submarine. 1". $200.

#43. End of Day, Submarine. 27/32". $2000.

END OF DAY SUBMARINE

Up to:		9.9-9.7	9.6-9.3	9.2-9.0	8.9-8.5	8.4-8.0	7.9-7.0
5/8"	High	80.00	40.00	38.00	28.00	NA	NA
	Low	31.00	40.00	35.00	28.00	NA	NA
	Average	49.25	40.00	36.50	28.00	NA	NA
	Quantity	4	1	2	1	0	0
3/4"	High	180.00	155.00	160.00	35.00	NA	37.00
	Low	105.00	85.00	30.00	35.00	NA	37.00
	Average	132.50	106.00	91.91	35.00	NA	37.00
	Quantity	4	5	12	1	0	1
1"	High	575.00	NA	NA	NA	NA	70.00
	Low	300.00	NA	NA	NA	NA	70.00
	Average	366.67	NA	NA	NA	NA	70.00
	Quantity	3	0	0	0	0	1
1-1/4"	High	400.00	NA	NA	NA	NA	80.00
	Low	400.00	NA	NA	NA	NA	80.00
	Average	400.00	NA	NA	NA	NA	80.00
	Quantity	1	0	0	0	0	1
1-1/2"	High	NA	NA	625.00	NA	NA	NA
	Low	NA	NA	625.00	NA	NA	NA
	Average	NA	NA	625.00	NA	NA	NA
	Quantity	0	0	1	0	0	0

MIST

A mist is a transparent or translucent base with colored flecks of transparent or translucent glass stretched on the surface or just below it. The stretched colors can form bands or can completely cover the marble. However, the colors must be transparent or translucent, so that light shines through the marble.

Usually, the base glass is transparent clear. However, other colored bases exist. These are rarer than the clear base. The outer layer is usually colored, although examples of a colored base with clear mist have been found.

Occasionally, there is mica just below the surface of the marble. This is fairly rare.

#44. Mist. 11/16". $50.   #45. Mist. 11/16". $50.

Mists

Up to:		9.9-9.7	9.6-9.3	9.2-9.0	8.9-8.5	8.4-8.0	7.9-7.0
5/8"	High	60.00	NA	50.00	10.00	NA	NA
	Low	27.00	NA	17.00	10.00	NA	NA
	Average	39.67	NA	32.75	10.00	NA	NA
	Quantity	4	0	4	1	0	0
7/8"	High	67.00	30.00	30.00	33.00	18.50	NA
	Low	42.00	17.00	25.00	8.00	11.00	NA
	Average	50.80	23.50	27.67	21.50	14.16	NA
	Quantity	5	2	3	9	3	0

SUBMARINE

A submarine is a difficult marble to categorize. They are a cross between an end of day panelled onionskin, an indian, a mist, and a banded swirl.

The base glass is always transparent, either clear or colored (usually blue or green). There are two end of day panels of stretched colored flecks on the surface of the marble. These panels are on opposite sides and usually each covers about one-quarter of the marble. In the two resultant clear panels, there are stretched colored flecks below the surface of the marble. This creates a multi-layer effect.

Occasionally, there is mica just below the surface of the marble or in the panels or bands of mica, which is even rarer.

#46. Submarine. 23/32". $450.   #47. Submarine. 7/8". $900.

Submarines

Up to:		9.9-9.7	9.6-9.3	9.2-9.0	8.9-8.5	8.4-8.0	7.9-7.0
5/8"	High	NA	220.00	NA	80.00	NA	NA
	Low	NA	220.00	NA	45.00	NA	NA
	Average	NA	220.00	NA	62.50	NA	NA
	Quantity	0	1	0	2	0	0
3/4"	High	455.00	400.00	NA	NA	NA	NA
	Low	455.00	400.00	NA	NA	NA	NA
	Average	455.00	400.00	NA	NA	NA	NA
	Quantity	1	1	0	0	0	0
7/8"	High	1550.00	NA	235.00	NA	NA	21.00
	Low	1550.00	NA	235.00	NA	NA	21.00
	Average	1550.00	NA	235.00	NA	NA	21.00
	Quantity	1	0	1	0	0	1

MICA

A mica marble is a transparent base glass with mica flakes in it. The most common colors are clear, blue, aqua, brown, and green. Olive green and smoky gray are less common. Amethyst is rare. Yellow is rarer. Red micas are not quite as rare as yellow, but are valued higher, probably because they are prettier.

Some micas have ghost cores (cores of tiny air bubbles) or thin dark filaments. These are odd, but do not seem to add greatly to the value of the marble. Single-pontil, multi-layer, cased, single-gather or end-of-cane marbles are very rare and are valued higher.

#48. Mica. 3/4". $30.

#49. Mica. 3/4". $25.

Micas

Up to:		9.9-9.7	9.6-9.3	9.2-9.0	8.9-8.5	8.4-8.0	7.9-7.0
1/2"	High	85.00	45.00	10.50	23.00	18.06	NA
	Low	7.00	10.00	5.00	1.00	3.50	NA
	Average	20.00	23.60	8.75	11.44	8.44	NA
	Quantity	35	5	6	11	7	0
5/8"	High	95.00	50.00	42.00	15.00	10.50	4.00
	Low	7.00	5.00	2.00	2.00	0.50	1.00
	Average	21.49	24.75	10.78	5.03	5.21	2.00
	Quantity	57	12	18	16	11.00	3
3/4"	High	200.00	21.00	80.00	40.00	16.50	12.00
	Low	7.00	7.00	4.00	2.00	3.00	2.00
	Average	34.61	14.21	23.08	9.24	6.61	5.63
	Quantity	54	7	28	22	9	4
7/8"	High	350.00	53.00	60.00	80.00	35.00	8.00
	Low	19.00	17.00	12.00	5.00	5.00	8.00
	Average	61.54	31.95	27.47	20.76	18.04	8.00
	Quantity	36	10	28	44	9	1
1"	High	NA	NA	170.00	75.00	55.00	30.00
	Low	NA	NA	27.00	19.00	12.00	30.00
	Average	NA	NA	54.60	38.80	37.66	30.00
	Quantity	0	0	11	5	6	1
1-1/4"	High	NA	NA	230.00	NA	NA	31.00
	Low	NA	NA	230.00	NA	NA	31.00
	Average	NA	NA	230.00	NA	NA	31.00
	Quantity	0	0	1	0	0	1
1-1/2"	High	NA	NA	NA	190.00	171.00	140.00
	Low	NA	NA	NA	190.00	171.00	75.00
	Average	NA	NA	NA	190.00	171.00	107.50
	Quantity	0	0	0	1	1	2

SLAG

A slag is a marble that is made from a cane that is a mixture of white glass mixed with black, purple, green, brown, or yellow glass. Rather than being a layered cane, like a Swirl, slags are drawn off of a cane that is a mixture of two colors. Single pontil examples will be covered in the transitional section.

#50. Slag. 19/32". $40.

Slags

Up to:		9.9-9.7	9.6-9.3	9.2-9.0	8.9-8.5	8.4-8.0	7.9-7.0
5/8"	High	NA	NA	NA	4.00	NA	NA
	Low	NA	NA	NA	4.00	NA	NA
	Average	NA	NA	NA	4.00	NA	NA
	Quantity	0	0	0	1	0	0
3/4"	High	80.00	NA	65.00	27.00	NA	NA
	Low	50.00	NA	40.00	15.00	NA	NA
	Average	65.00	NA	52.50	21.00	NA	NA
	Quantity	2	0	2	2	0	0
7/8"	High	NA	NA	35.00	24.00	NA	13.00
	Low	NA	NA	35.00	24.00	NA	12.00
	Average	NA	NA	35.00	24.00	NA	12.50
	Quantity	0	0	1	1	0	2
1"	High	NA	NA	NA	NA	NA	NA
	Low	NA	NA	NA	NA	NA	NA
	Average	NA	NA	NA	NA	NA	NA
	Quantity	0	0	0	0	0	0
1-1/4"	High	NA	NA	NA	160.00	NA	55.00
	Low	NA	NA	NA	160.00	NA	55.00
	Average	NA	NA	NA	160.00	NA	55.00
	Quantity	0	0	0	1	0	1

OPAQUE

An opaque marble is made from a rod of a single opaque color. White and black are the most common colors. Blue, pink, and green are rarer. Other opaque or translucent colors are even rarer. Single pontil marbles, either single-gather or end-of-cane are very rare.

There is also a type of opaque that is made from a rod of two opaque or translucent colors. The rod had one color (usually semi-opaque white) on one side and another color (usually semi-opaque green or blue) on the other. When the marble was twisted off the end, one side of the marble is one color and the other side is the other color. Because of the twisting motion, the marble looks like a machine-made corkscrew, but has two pontils, hence the name "handmade corkscrew." These are very rare.

#51. Opaque. 11/16". $20.

Opaques

Up to:		9.9-9.7	9.6-9.3	9.2-9.0	8.9-8.5	8.4-8.0	7.9-7.0
1/2"	High	33.25	27.00	NA	1.00	NA	NA
	Low	31.00	27.00	NA	1.00	NA	NA
	Average	32.13	27.00	NA	1.00	NA	NA
	Quantity	2	1	0	1	0	0
5/8"	High	35.40	50.00	12.00	22.00	NA	NA
	Low	11.00	6.00	12.00	5.00	NA	NA
	Average	30.79	29.33	12.00	10.65	NA	NA
	Quantity	30	3	1	10	0	0
3/4"	High	NA	NA	27.00	37.00	16.39	NA
	Low	NA	NA	17.50	2.00	4.00	NA
	Average	NA	NA	22.25	10.19	7.80	NA
	Quantity	0	0	2	12	4	0
7/8"	High	75.00	NA	40.00	45.00	NA	NA
	Low	25.00	NA	38.99	13.00	NA	NA
	Average	50.00	NA	39.33	29.00	NA	NA
	Quantity	2	0	3	2	0	0
1"	High	NA	NA	NA	160.00	20.00	NA
	Low	NA	NA	NA	160.00	20.00	NA
	Average	NA	NA	NA	160.00	20.00	NA
	Quantity	0	0	0	1	1	0

CLEARIE

A clearie marble is made from a rod of a single transparent color. Clear is the most common, although light blue, light green, and light amber examples are known. Single pontil examples, either single-gather or end-of-cane, are rarer.

#52. Clearie. 11/16". $20.

Clearies

Up to:		9.9-9.7	9.6-9.3	9.2-9.0	8.9-8.5	8.4-8.0	7.9-7.0
5/8"	High	15.00	NA	NA	NA	3.00	NA
	Low	7.00	NA	NA	NA	2.00	NA
	Average	9.66	NA	NA	NA	2.66	NA
	Quantity	6	0	0	0	3	0
3/4"	High	29.00	NA	60.00	15.00	4.00	3.00
	Low	29.00	NA	5.00	5.00	3.00	3.00
	Average	29.00	NA	22.21	10.00	3.50	3.00
	Quantity	1	0	19	2	2	1

SULPHIDE

A sulphide has a transparent base with a ceramic-type figure inserted inside it. They are single-gather, single-pontil marbles.

The most common figure that is found in sulphide marbles is an animal. Barnyard animals, household pets, squirrels, and birds are most common. Wild animals including razorbacks, elephants, and lions are a little less common.

Human figures are more difficult to find. These can be either full length figures or busts.

There is a series of sulphide marbles that contain the individual numerals 0 to 9. There are also sulphide marbles with figures of inanimate objects in them. These are usually coins, numerals on disks or pocket watches. They are extremely rare.

Some sulphide figures are painted. We have seen figures that are painted (simply or elaborately), as well as numerals and inanimate objects that are painted. The value of these is greatly affected by the degree of coverage, the brightness of the colors, and the number of colors used.

A very few sulphide figures have been found in transparent colored glass. A number of shades have been found, including blues, greens, yellows, amethysts, browns, and pinks. These are very rare.

Also, extremely few sulphides have been found with more than one figure in them. These are also extremely rare.

The value of a sulphide is greatly affected by several factors, other than the type of figure in the marble. Because the figures were inserted into the glass by hand, the skill of the maker greatly affected the quality of the marble.

Figures that are off-center in the marble can be greatly discounted in value (by as much as 50%). A figure can either be too close to the right or left side of the marble, too high or low, or set too far forward or back.

The figure had to be heated to the same temperature as the glass on the end of the punty, in order for the marble to be made properly. If the temperature difference between the glass and the figure was too great, then the marble would shatter when it was being made. In some cases, the temperature difference was not so great that the marble would shatter, but rather the figure would crack when inserted. Cracked figures discount the value of the marble (by up to 50%). In other cases, pieces of the figure broke off when it was inserted into the glass. This also discounts the value.

In some cases, as the figure was being inserted into the marble, some air would be trapped in the marble as well. A thin layer of trapped air around the figure was necessary to achieve a silvery sheen that enhances the viewing of the figure. However, too much trapped air can cause so much reflection that the figure cannot be properly seen. Trapped air can discount the value of the marble by as much as 60%.

Finally, because sulphides are single-pontil marbles, there is always one pontil on the surface, that in some cases is ground down. If the pontil is on the bottom pole of the marble, then the figure can be viewed properly from all angles. However, depending on the skill of the maker, the pontil could end up anywhere on the marble in relation to the figure. In some instances, the pontil obscures viewing the figure. This can result in a discount on the value of the marble (up to 40%).

In 1993, a group of sulphides surfaced that have become the source of great controversy in the marble collecting community. These marbles have been dubbed "California Sulphides" because there was only one person who was selling them, and he was from California. Without getting into the whole history of the events surrounding the introduction of these marbles to the market, it is safe to say that the marble collecting community has been pretty much divided as to whether these marbles are as old as traditionally known sulphides, or are modern reproductions, or are older but not as old as antique sulphides. You must reach your own conclusions as to the age of these marbles.

They can be identified by several features. Many of them were in colored glass (usually very dark) or a light vaseline color. Many contained multiple figures (two or more). Many were figures that had never been seen before (seahorse, lady riding a horse side-saddle, etc.). None of the figures had a silvery sheen to them, and many had a light rust-red haze on them. Very few of the marbles fluoresced under a black light (traditional sulphides usually fluoresce). Many had either a polished surface or an unpolished surface that had many tiny fissures in it when viewed by a 10x lens.

At this point, no one has been able to definitively prove that these marbles are new or old. You must draw your own conclusions.

#53. Sulphide. 1-3/4". $110.

#54. Sulphide. 1-5/8". $300.

#55. Sulphide. 1-5/8". $3000.

#56. Sulphide. 1-1/2". $3000.

Sulphides

Up to:		9.9-9.7	9.6-9.3	9.2-9.0	8.9-8.5	8.4-8.0	7.9-7.0
1"	High	135.00	NA	NA	220.00	NA	NA
	Low	135.00	NA	NA	85.00	NA	NA
	Average	135.00	NA	NA	152.50	NA	NA
	Quantity	1	0	0	2	0	0
1-1/4"	High	140.00	400.00	335.00	635.00	310.00	32.00
	Low	80.00	330.00	75.00	38.00	55.00	32.00
	Average	105.00	366.67	173.33	165.46	143.33	32.00
	Quantity	4	3	3	13	3	1
1-1/2"	High	155.00	350.00	110.00	410.00	300.00	250.00
	Low	155.00	95.00	65.00	36.00	32.00	17.00
	Average	155.00	180.00	85.00	129.61	78.89	65.11
	Quantity	1	4	4	13	18	9
1-3/4"	High	100.00	675.00	1000.00	550.00	360.00	235.00
	Low	100.00	380.00	80.00	40.00	55.00	22.00
	Average	100.00	527.20	290.42	170.20	146.22	63.66
	Quantity	2	2	12	10	17	12
2"	High	725.00	NA	140.00	1100.00	267.50	400.00
	Low	355.00	NA	55.00	75.00	80.00	39.00
	Average	540.00	NA	97.29	248.33	217.50	183.50
	Quantity	2	0	15	23	6	5
2-1/4"	High	NA	NA	240.00	95.00	140.00	103.50
	Low	NA	NA	240.00	95.00	100.00	55.00
	Average	NA	NA	240.00	95.00	120.00	82.83
	Quantity	0	0	1	1	2	3
2-1/2"	High	NA	NA	130.00	110.00	NA	NA
	Low	NA	NA	130.00	60.00	NA	NA
	Average	NA	NA	130.00	85.00	NA	NA
	Quantity	0	0	1	2	0	0

OTHER SINGLE-GATHER

Most varieties of cane-cut handmade marbles can also be found as single-pontil marbles. However, almost all of these are end-of-cane marbles, not single-gather marbles. A single-gather marble is a marble that was produced one at a time by adding successive layers of glass onto the end of a punty.

Several types of cane-cut marbles were also produced as single-gather marbles. These are End of Day Clouds, Micas, and Opaques. However, the single-gather versions are much rarer than the cane-cut versions.

PAPERWEIGHT/CONFETTI

A Paperweight marble is a transparent glass base with small flecks or chips of colored glass forming a layer near the pontil of the marble. The marbles are rare. Almost all have a transparent clear base. I have only seen one with a transparent colored base, and that one was blue. The colored flecks are usually white, pink, yellow or green. I have only seen them in 9/16" to 3/4" size. Larger sizes are very rare, if they exist at all. A second type has four vanes of glass bits similar in design to a cat's-eye.

A rarer type of paperweight marble has a layer of millefiori canes where you would normally find the flecks of glass.

#57. Non-Glass Handmade, Paperweight. 15/16". $1500.

Paperweight/Confetti

Up to:		9.9-9.7	9.6-9.3	9.2-9.0	8.9-8.5	8.4-8.0	7.9-7.0
5/8"	High	110.00	NA	65.00	NA	NA	NA
	Low	110.00	NA	26.00	NA	NA	NA
	Average	110.00	NA	45.50	NA	NA	NA
	Quantity	1	0	2	0	0	0
3/4"	High	100.00	NA	NA	NA	NA	NA
	Low	85.00	NA	NA	NA	NA	NA
	Average	92.50	NA	NA	NA	NA	NA
	Quantity	2	0	0	0	0	0
1"	High	700.00	NA	NA	NA	NA	NA
	Low	700.00	NA	NA	NA	NA	NA
	Average	700.00	NA	NA	NA	NA	NA
	Quantity	1	0	0	0	0	0
		vaned					
1-1/2"	High	2250.00	NA	NA	1200.00	NA	NA
	Low	2250.00	NA	NA	1200.00	NA	NA
	Average	2250.00	NA	NA	1200.00	NA	NA
	Quantity	1	0	0	1	0	0
		millefiori			millefiori		

HANDMADE NON-GLASS MARBLES

Serious collectors of handmade non-glass marbles are few and far between. Other than having one or two examples of each type in their collections, most collectors do not want these marbles. This is no doubt because, quite frankly, most of the marbles are quite plain.

Clay and bennington marbles were produced by the millions, in both Germany and the United States, during the late 1800s and early 1900s. They were easy and cheap to produce, not requiring the technical knowledge or skill of glass marbles. The first marbles produced in the United States were clay marbles and the first marble-related U.S. patents are for devices that "mass produce" clay marbles.

While clays and benningtons are not in great demand, collectors are more interested in hand-painted china marbles and agates. Some of the hand-painted chinas are very colorful and beautiful. No marble collection is complete without a sampling. Hand-painted chinas can also be quite rare. Scenic chinas rival most handmade glass marbles in terms of the price for rare examples.

No marble collection is complete without a sampling of hand-cut agates either. These marbles were the choice of marble shooters for many years, because of their ability to knock glass marbles out of the ring. Many hand-cut agates exhibit exquisite and complicated natural designs. A fine collection of different hand-cut agates could be created.

Another choice of some marble players was the steelie. These were preferred by players because their density could easily knock glass marbles out of a ring. However, they were banned from tournament play. Many steelies are merely ball bearings, but some are handmade hollow spheres that required a great deal of time to make. Every collection should have at least one handmade steelie.

In reality, handmade non-glass marbles do not get much attention by marble collectors. These marbles tend to get caught in the shuffle of the pursuit for the prettier and more colorful glass marbles. However, you should take your time and look at them while building your collection. They were an important part of the game of marbles for years and some of them are actually quite attractive.

CLAY

Clay marbles are the most common old marble that you will find. These marbles were the easiest to produce and hundreds of thousands, probably millions, still exist. Unfortunately, clay marbles do not have nearly the eye-appeal of any other marbles and therefore are the least collectible of any marble.

Clay marbles were made in both Germany and the United States. It has been reported that clay marbles were used as ballast in the keels of ships that sailed to America from Germany, and were then removed and sold in this country. On the American side, some of the earliest U.S. marble-related patents are for devices that fashion blobs of clay into round spheres, which were then fired to harden them.

Clay marbles are usually found in their natural tan color, but they may also be dyed. The dyed marbles are usually found in red, blue, brown, green or yellow. Foil clays are small (usually less than 1/2" diameter) clays with a metallic coating on them. These were produced in Germany after the turn of the century and are usually found in Mosaic games. None of these clays are very collectible because they are so common.

#58. Non-Glass Handmade, Clay. 9/16". $0.10 each.

Clay

Up to:		9.9-9.7	9.6-9.3	9.2-9.0	8.9-8.5	8.4-8.0	7.9-7.0
1/2"	High	0.17	NA	NA	NA	NA	NA
	Low	0.01	NA	NA	NA	NA	NA
	Average	0.03	NA	NA	NA	NA	NA
	Quantity	136	0	0	0	0	0
5/8"	High	0.12	NA	NA	NA	NA	NA
	Low	0.01	NA	NA	NA	NA	NA
	Average	0.02	NA	NA	NA	NA	NA
	Quantity	545	0	0	0	0	0
1"	High	9.00	NA	NA	NA	NA	NA
	Low	0.07	NA	NA	NA	NA	NA
	Average	0.56	NA	NA	NA	NA	NA
	Quantity	58	0	0	0	0	0
1-1/2"	High	22.00	NA	NA	NA	NA	NA
	Low	1.13	NA	NA	NA	NA	NA
	Average	4.83	NA	NA	NA	NA	NA
	Quantity	22	0	0	0	0	0

CROCKERY

Crockery marbles are a type of clay marble that is made from two or three different colors of clay. Some are merely opaque white or off-white marbles that were fired at a higher temperature than clays, making them somewhat denser. There are also some lined crockery that are opaque white with thin blue and/or green swirls mixed in. These are rarer and somewhat collectible.

The lined crockery marbles were made by rolling together different colors of clay. You can achieve the same effect today with a little experimentation with Sculpty®

clay. Crockery marbles were all fired to harden them. There are glazed and un-glazed varieties of crockery marbles. Some have very intricate designs in the swirl patterns. They are more collectible than clays, and have been showing increased interest in the last year.

#59. Non-Glass Hand-made, Crockery. 3/4".
$50.

#60. Non-Glass Hand-made, Crockery. 3/4".
$30.

Crockery

Up to:		9.9-9.7	9.6-9.3	9.2-9.0	8.9-8.5	8.4-8.0	7.9-7.0
5/8"	High	3.00	6.00	1.00	NA	NA	NA
	Low	1.00	2.00	1.00	NA	NA	NA
	Average	2.00	3.33	1.00	NA	NA	NA
	Quantity	2	3	1	0	0	0
3/4"	High	16.50	9.00	2.00	6.00	NA	NA
	Low	7.00	4.00	2.00	6.00	NA	NA
	Average	11.83	5.55	2.00	6.00	NA	NA
	Quantity	3	5	1	1	0	0
1"	High	11.50	55.00	47.00	NA	NA	NA
	Low	8.00	37.00	27.00	NA	NA	NA
	Average	9.75	46.00	39.67	NA	NA	NA
	Quantity	2	2	3	0	0	0
1-1/4"	High	14.00	96.00	NA	NA	NA	NA
	Low	14.00	8.00	NA	NA	NA	NA
	Average	14.00	49.50	NA	NA	NA	NA
	Quantity	1	4	0	0	0	0

BENNINGTON

Bennington marbles are a type of glazed clay marble. They are not very dense. The marbles are fired clay with a salt glaze on them. Benningtons are readily iden-tifiable by both their coloring and the little "eyes" that they have on them. These are spots where the marbles were touching each other while they were being fired, resulting in those spots being uncolored and unglazed.

The term "Bennington" is actually a misnomer. There is no evidence that they were ever made in Bennington, Vermont, or that they have any lineage to the

Bennington pottery that they resemble and from which they get their name. It appears that all Bennington marbles were imported from Germany. Some boxes have been found that contain them and that are labeled "Agates - Imitation / Made in Germany."

Benningtons are usually colored brown or blue. Marbles that have both brown and blue on them, as well as a little green, are referred to as "fancy Benningtons". These are rarer than the single color variety. There are also some very rare examples with pink on them.

#61. Non-Glass Handmade, Bennington. 3/4". $10.

#62. Non-Glass Handmade, Bennington. 19/32". $50.

Bennington

Up to:		9.9-9.7	9.6-9.3	9.2-9.0	8.9-8.5	8.4-8.0	7.9-7.0
1"	High	15.00	8.00	19.00	NA	NA	NA
	Low	8.00	8.00	2.00	NA	NA	NA
	Average	11.05	8.00	7.00	NA	NA	NA
	Quantity	8	1	4	0	0	0
1-1/4"	High	22.00	7.50	NA	NA	NA	NA
	Low	7.00	7.00	NA	NA	NA	NA
	Average	13.46	7.25	NA	NA	NA	NA
	Quantity	7	2	0	0	0	0

STONEWARE

Stoneware marbles are a dense, fired clay marble with salt glaze on them. These marbles are made in the same manner as salt-glazed stoneware crocks and jugs and may very well have been made by the same makers. The marbles have similar blue patterns on them. Usually the patterns are spongeware-type or splatterware-type, or else they tend to be bands encircling the equator.

These marbles are fairly rare, although not very collectible, because of their lack of eye appeal.

#63. Non-Glass Hand-made, Stoneware. 1". $50.

#64. Non-Glass Handmade, Stoneware. 1-1/4". $75.

Stoneware

Up to:		9.9-9.7	9.6-9.3	9.2-9.0	8.9-8.5	8.4-8.0	7.9-7.0
1-3/8"	High	NA	55.00	NA	NA	NA	NA
	Low	NA	50.00	NA	NA	NA	NA
	Average	NA	52.50	NA	NA	NA	NA
	Quantity	0	2	0	0	0	0
1-7/8"	High	110.00	75.00	NA	NA	NA	NA
	Low	110.00	50.00	NA	NA	NA	NA
	Average	110.00	63.33	NA	NA	NA	NA
	Quantity	1	3	0	0	0	0

CHINA

China marbles are marbles that are made with a very dense white clay and then fired at a very high temperature. This produces a much heavier marble, for the size, than a clay or crockery marble. Most chinas are painted. Some of the decorations can be quite intricate. Many of the chinas that you will find are glazed as well. Jeff Carskadden has written an excellent book on china marbles (see bibliography) and you should refer to it for a more detailed description of the different types.

In order of rarity, painted chinas have the following patterns: Lines on one axis, helix on pole or poles, intersecting lines, crows feet, bull's-eyes, simple flowers, donut hole flowers, roses, intricate roses, scenic designs. Some hand-painted chinas have been found with gold-colored bull's-eyes. These are rare.

#65. Non-Glass Handmade, China. 3/4". $40.

#66. Non-Glass Handmade, China. 11/16". $15.

#67. Non-Glass Handmade, China. 23/32". $35.

#68. Non-Glass Handmade, China. 1-1/8". $3500.

China

Up to:		9.9-9.7	9.6-9.3	9.2-9.0	8.9-8.5	8.4-8.0	7.9-7.0
1/2"	High	NA	1.00	NA	NA	NA	NA
	Low	NA	1.00	NA	NA	NA	NA
	Average	NA	1.00	NA	NA	NA	NA
	Quantity	0	1	0	0	0	0
5/8"	High	25.00	40.00	7.00	NA	NA	NA
	Low	1.00	1.00	3.00	NA	NA	NA
	Average	14.91	8.42	5.00	NA	NA	NA
	Quantity	22	11	3	0	0	0
3/4"	High	73.00	42.00	35.00	NA	NA	NA
	Low	1.00	1.00	2.00	NA	NA	NA
	Average	16.84	12.20	11.69	NA	NA	NA
	Quantity	14	11	9	0	0	0
7/8"	High	75.00	75.00	23.00	47.00	NA	NA
	Low	1.00	6.00	23.00	15.00	NA	NA
	Average	26.29	43.50	23.00	26.33	NA	NA
	Quantity	12	8	1	3	0	0
1"	High	NA	150.00	15.00	NA	NA	NA
	Low	NA	4.00	15.00	NA	NA	NA
	Average	NA	62.58	15.00	NA	NA	NA
	Quantity	0	6	1	0	0	0
1-1/4"	High	700.00	155.00	55.00	36.00	NA	NA
	Low	22.00	30.00	11.00	36.00	NA	NA
	Average	182.50	92.09	22.40	36.00	NA	NA
	Quantity	8	2	5	1	0	0
1-1/2"	High	160.00	385.00	4200.00	55.00	NA	NA
	Low	160.00	12.00	4200.00	55.00	NA	NA
	Average	160.00	102.67	4200.00	55.00	NA	NA
	Quantity	1	6	1	1	0	0

CARPET BALL

Carpet balls are glazed crockery spheres that are used in a game similar to bocce. Most carpet balls are believed to have been made in England or Scotland, where the game was very popular.

Most carpet balls are in the 3" to 3-1/2" range. They have varying designs painted on them. Some of the designs (from most common to least common) are: Lined, intersecting lines-single color, intersecting lines-multiple colors, crown and thistle, flower, and mochaware. Mochaware tend to be slightly smaller. There is a small sized (about 2-1/4") opaque white ball that is called the jack. This was the target ball. Sometimes, the name of a store is printed on them. There were also child-size balls (about 2-1/2"). These are less common.

Recently, many reproductions have begun to appear. These can be identified by several features: They have a thick clear glaze; many have small circular hit marks that just crack the glaze; and, if they have small chips, then the interior is a dark white or tan color (original carpet balls have chalky white interiors).

#69. Non-Glass Hand-made, Carpet Ball. 3-1/4". $100.

#70. Non-Glass Hand-made, Carpet Ball. 3-1/4". $100.

#71. Non-Glass Hand-made, Mochaware. 2-3/4". $600.

Carpet Balls

Up to:		9.9-9.7	9.6-9.3	9.2-9.0	8.9-8.5	8.4-8.0	7.9-7.0
1-3/8"	High	NA	NA	75.00	NA	NA	31.00
	Low	NA	NA	66.00	NA	NA	31.00
	Average	NA	NA	70.33	NA	NA	31.00
	Quantity	0	0	3	0	0	1
2"	High	150.00	150.00	NA	49.00	NA	NA
	Low	150.00	150.00	NA	49.00	NA	NA
	Average	150.00	150.00	NA	49.00	NA	NA
	Quantity	1	2	0	1	0	0
2-1/2"	High	NA	NA	160.00	63.00	23.00	NA
	Low	NA	NA	160.00	42.00	20.00	NA
	Average	NA	NA	160.00	51.50	21.50	NA
	Quantity	0	0	1	2	2	0

AGATE

Agate is a colored variety of quartz that was hand-ground into marbles. They were a favorite of many marble players, especially as shooters. This is because agates are denser than other marbles. This made it easier to knock an opponent's marble out of the ring.

Hand-cut agates are generally found in banded and carnelian varieties. The banded varieties have distinct concentric rings on the sphere. They command a value that is about double the carnelian examples. Carnelians are a more uniform brownish-red color. Many agate marbles have subsurface moons because of their extensive use as shooters.

There are many machine-ground agates available. These are modern. Hand-cut agates have tiny facets on the surface. You can see the light dance on the surface if you look closely at the surface while turning the marble. There are also dyed agates available. Some of these are older, hand-cuts and some are modern. A chemical process is used to accentuate the brightness of the natural colors. Usually they are found in green, blue, and black and occasionally in yellow.

#72. Non-Glass Handmade, Agate. 1". $150.

#73. Non-Glass Handmade, Agate. 5/8" to 11/16". $5-10 each.

Agates

Up to:		9.9-9.7	9.6-9.3	9.2-9.0	8.9-8.5	8.4-8.0	7.9-7.0
1/2"	High	19.00	19.00	5.00	2.00	NA	NA
	Low	2.00	19.00	5.00	2.00	NA	NA
	Average	7.43	19.00	5.00	2.00	NA	NA
	Quantity	7	1	1	1	0	0
5/8"	High	27.00	NA	NA	12.00	NA	NA
	Low	2.00	NA	NA	0.50	NA	NA
	Average	9.11	NA	NA	5.08	NA	NA
	Quantity	9	0	0	6	0	0
3/4"	High	40.00	160.00	43.22	8.00	NA	NA
	Low	6.00	5.00	4.00	2.00	NA	NA
	Average	19.72	26.39	18.75	3.81	NA	NA
	Quantity	16	24	8	4	0	0
1"	High	55.00	49.00	15.00	29.00	8.00	NA
	Low	10.00	20.00	7.00	10.00	5.00	NA
	Average	25.17	34.50	10.80	18.50	6.33	NA
	Quantity	17	2	5	4	3	0
1-1/4"	High	46.00	50.00	NA	NA	NA	NA
	Low	46.00	37.00	NA	NA	NA	NA
	Average	46.00	43.50	NA	NA	NA	NA
	Quantity	1	2	0	0	0	0
1-1/2"	High	75.00	NA	32.00	27.00	NA	NA
	Low	56.00	NA	32.00	27.00	NA	NA
	Average	65.50	NA	32.00	27.00	NA	NA
	Quantity	2	0	1	1	0	0

OTHER MATERIALS

Handmade marbles were also produced from wood and from steel. Wooden marbles can be found in either their natural color or dyed. They were probably not used in marble playing because they are not very dense, and therefore not very effective for shooting or targets. Few collectors collect them, and the author could locate no sales records for them during this period of time.

STEELIE

Marble collectors come across a number of steel marbles in their hunting. Most of these are solid ball bearings. These have no real value to marble collectors.

However, there are some handmade steelies available. These are hollow steel spheres that were made by hand. They can be identified by their lightness and by the "X" on one end where the open end was folded. Occasionally, they may have rust, but clean examples are collectible. Larger hollow steelies are very rare.

#74. Non-Glass Handmade, Steelie. 11/16". $15.

Steelie

Up to:		9.9-9.7	9.6-9.3	9.2-9.0	8.9-8.5	8.4-8.0	7.9-7.0
5/8"	High	15.00	NA	9.00	NA	NA	NA
	Low	8.00	NA	8.00	NA	NA	NA
	Average	11.50	NA	8.50	NA	NA	NA
	Quantity	6	0	2	0	0	0
1"	High	27.00	NA	NA	NA	NA	NA
	Low	17.00	NA	NA	NA	NA	NA
	Average	22.00	NA	NA	NA	NA	NA
	Quantity	3	0	0	0	0	0

PAPER MACHE

There is also a type of marble that seems to be constructed from paper mache. These are very rare. They are very light and were probably meant for use in a board game and not in marble shooting games. The marbles are various combinations of red, black, orange, and yellow, in a swirled pattern.

While these marbles are still referred to as Paper Mache, there is evidence that they are in fact Gutta Perche (an early type of rubber).

#75. Non-Glass Handmade,
Paper Mache. 7/8". $250.

Paper Mache

Up to: 7/8"		9.9-9.7	9.6-9.3	9.2-9.0	8.9-8.5	8.4-8.0	7.9-7.0
	High	350.00	130.00	NA	160.00	23.00	NA
	Low	275.00	130.00	NA	51.00	23.00	NA
	Average	312.50	130.00	NA	103.66	23.00	NA
	Quantity	2	1	0	3	1	0
1"	High	370.00	200.00	NA	NA	NA	NA
	Low	310.00	150.00	NA	NA	NA	NA
	Average	340.00	177.85	NA	NA	NA	NA
	Quantity	2	7	0	0	0	0

MACHINE-MADE MARBLES

Until about fifteen years ago, machine-made marbles were not considered collectible by many marble collectors. Most collectors ended up with machine-made marbles as part of collections that they were buying because they wanted the handmade marbles in them. They would generally throw the machine-made marbles in a box and forget about them. Very little attempt was made to identify or classify the many different types of machine-made marbles, either by appearance or by manufacturer. There were some notable exceptions to this, especially in the area of Akro Agate Company or Peltier Glass Company marbles. But, for the most part, machine-made marbles were not given much serious attention by the majority of collectors.

For several reasons, all of that began to change during the mid-1980s. An influx of new collectors into the hobby created a demand for handmade marbles that had not previously existed. This increased the prices of handmade marbles. As those prices began to move up at a rapid rate, collectors found that they could acquire many beautiful and colorful machine-made marbles for the price of a single handmade marble.

Another reason that machine-made marbles began to receive more attention was related to their historical significance. Virtually all handmade marbles were made in Germany and then imported into the United States (as well as other countries). Machine-made marbles were almost exclusively an American product for the first half of the twentieth century. The rise of American marble manufacturers mirrors in many ways the rise of the United States as an economic force. Many examples of original packaging still exist, making it easy to identify the different types and manufacturers of machine-made marbles. An interest arose in documenting and preserving this period of American toy manufacturing.

The final reason for the increased interest in machine-made marbles was nostalgia. By the mid-1980s, the kids who had played with mibs, aggies, and commies in the playground had grown up. As occurred with many other collectibles over the past two decades, collectors began buying back the objects of their youth that had been lost to numerous location changes or indifference.

So, by the late 1980s, the time and environment were ripe for an explosion of interest in machine-made marbles. The catalyst for this explosion was the publication in 1990 of the book *Collectable Machine Made Marbles* by Larry Castle and Marlowe Peterson. Previously (since 1976), the Marble Collectors Society of America had published identification sheets and prices for machine-made marbles, but the Castle and Peterson book was the first attempt to classify all types of machine-made marbles by manufacturer.

Since the publication of the Castle and Peterson book, the number of people collecting machine-made marbles has grown by leaps and bounds. This increased interest and demand has seen the publication of several additional books on machine-made marbles or their manufacturers (see the bibliography for a complete list).

TRANSITIONAL

Transitional marbles are among the earliest American-made marbles. The term "transitional" applies to most slag-type marbles that have one pontil. These marbles were probably made by one of several processes. Some were made by gathering a glob of molten glass from a pot onto the end of a punty and then either rounding a single marble off the end or allowing the glass to drip off the end of the punty into a machine as another worker cut the stream to create individual globs of glass. It is also likely that some later transitionals were actually made completely by machine. In this case, the stream of glass came out of a furnace, through a shearing mechanism, and then went into a crude set of rollers that rounded the marbles, but did not rotate them around all axes. As a result, the cut-off mark from the shearing mechanism remained.

These marbles are collectively called "transitional" because many were made partly by hand and partly by machine. Thus, they represent a bridge between handmade marbles and machine-made marbles.

Many "Regular Pontil" and "Ground Pontil" Transitionals were probably made in Germany from the period of about 1850 to 1920. Several American companies produced transitional marbles. Most of the companies were short-lived. Among the better known companies are Navarre Glass Company and M.F. Christensen & Son Company. It is very difficult to identify individual transitional marbles with specific companies. This is because very, very few have ever been found in their original packaging.

Transitional marbles are usually identified by the type of pontil. Some are also identified by the manufacturer, but this can be difficult, at best.

All transitionals are slag-type marbles. They are a colored transparent glass with translucent or opaque white mixed in. There are a few marbles that are a transparent clear glass with colors swirled in. These are commonly called "Leighton" marbles (#171) and are rare.

There are six basic types of pontil: Regular, Ground, Melted, Pinpoint, Fold, and Crease.

REGULAR PONTIL TRANSITIONAL

Regular pontil transitionals have a pontil on one end that looks just like the pontil on a handmade marble. This type is fairly rare. It is likely that many of these were not even made using any type of machine. Rather, they were individually hand-gathered on a punty and then rounded in a device and sheared off.

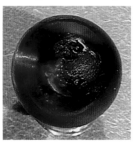

#77. Transition,
Regular Pontil.
27/32". $100.

#76. Transition,
Regular Pontil.
23/32". $75.

Regular Pontil Transitional

Up to:		9.9-9.7	9.6-9.3	9.2-9.0	8.9-8.5	8.4-8.0	7.9-7.0
5/8"	High	35.00	15.00	NA	NA	NA	NA
	Low	35.00	15.00	NA	NA	NA	NA
	Average	35.00	15.00	NA	NA	NA	NA
	Quantity	1	1	0	0	0	0
3/4"	High	40.00	27.00	30.00	29.00	NA	NA
	Low	35.00	15.00	14.00	11.00	NA	NA
	Average	39.91	21.74	22.00	20.00	NA	NA
	Quantity	6	8	2	2	0	0
7/8"	High	75.00	NA	NA	40.00	27.00	NA
	Low	75.00	NA	NA	20.00	8.00	NA
	Average	75.00	NA	NA	24.09	13.75	NA
	Quantity	1	0	0	7	4	0

GROUND PONTIL TRANSITIONAL

Ground pontil transitionals have a pontil on one end that has been ground and faceted. Many of these are Regular pontil transitionals that the manufacturer took the time to grind the pontil off of. They command about the same prices as Regular pontil transitionals, but they are not quite as rare. Some varieties of Ground pontil transitionals have oxblood and/or bright yellow or white swirled in. These are referred to as "Leighton" marbles), because it is popularly believed that an early marble-maker named James Leighton developed the colors used in these. The "Leighton" transitionals are very rare. Recently, some reproduction transitionals with oxblood have appeared. Please see the reproduction section of the guide for information on those marbles.

#78. Transition, Ground Pontil. 11/16". $30.

#79. Transition, Ground Pontil. 3/4". $250.

Ground Pontil Transitionals

Up to:		9.9-9.7	9.6-9.3	9.2-9.0	8.9-8.5	8.4-8.0	7.9-7.0
1/2"	High	37.00	NA	NA	NA	NA	NA
	Low	37.00	NA	NA	NA	NA	NA
	Average	37.00	NA	NA	NA	NA	NA
	Quantity	1	0	0	0	0	0
5/8"	High	50.00	26.00	50.00	22.00	17.00	NA
	Low	12.00	26.00	8.00	8.00	17.00	NA
	Average	21.15	26.00	19.07	13.33	17.00	NA
	Quantity	39	1	14	3	1	0
3/4"	High	85.00	100.00	37.00	50.00	NA	NA
	Low	19.50	12.00	15.00	7.00	NA	NA
	Average	39.45	37.38	24.38	17.60	NA	NA
	Quantity	41	21	8	5	0	0
7/8"	High	75.00	45.00	71.00	22.00	19.00	4.00
	Low	17.00	22.00	17.00	8.00	14.00	4.00
	Average	40.76	38.50	29.06	18.50	16.50	4.00
	Quantity	23	12	32	14	2	1
1"	High	NA	210.00	125.00	NA	NA	NA
	Low	NA	150.00	125.00	NA	NA	NA
	Average	NA	180.00	125.00	NA	NA	NA
	Quantity	0	2	1	0	0	0
1-1/4"	High	NA	NA	NA	145.00	NA	NA
	Low	NA	NA	NA	100.00	NA	NA
	Average	NA	NA	NA	122.50	NA	NA
	Quantity	0	0	0	2	0	0
1-1/2"	High	NA	NA	NA	190.00	NA	NA
	Low	NA	NA	NA	190.00	NA	NA
	Average	NA	NA	NA	190.00	NA	NA
	Quantity	0	0	0	1	0	0

MELTED PONTIL TRANSITIONAL

Melted pontil transitionals are more common than either Regular pontils or Ground pontils. These are marbles that have a pontil on one end that has been partially melted into the marble. The pontil was either melted manually over a flame or else was melted into the marble surface while the marble was being formed in the early marble-making machine. Most Melted Pontil Transitionals exhibit either a "9 and swirl pattern" or else a looping pattern where the white runs in a band or bands from the pole, over the top of the marble, and back to the pole. It is generally believed that the "9" pattern was made by the M.F. Christensen & Son Company and that the looping pattern was made by the Navarre Glass Company.

However, since the glass for these marbles was hand-gathered, it may very well be that they were simply made by different gatherers in the same factory. The "9" pattern marbles (marbles where the white glass on the top pole forms a "9") seem to be a little more common than the loop pattern marbles.

#80. Transition, Melted Pontil. 27/32". $35.

#81. Transition, Melted Pontil. 3/4". $30.

Melted Pontil Transitionals

Up to:		9.9-9.7	9.6-9.3	9.2-9.0	8.9-8.5	8.4-8.0	7.9-7.0
5/8"	High	42.00	21.00	15.00	13.09	NA	NA
	Low	20.00	14.00	15.00	3.00	NA	NA
	Average	23.14	16.50	15.00	8.10	NA	NA
	Quantity	7	5	1	6	0	0
3/4"	High	70.00	NA	22.50	15.00	13.00	NA
	Low	12.00	NA	8.00	3.00	11.00	NA
	Average	31.00	NA	11.84	10.25	12.00	NA
	Quantity	9	0	8	4	2	0
7/8"	High	60.00	65.00	NA	26.00	10.00	5.00
	Low	12.00	32.00	NA	10.00	5.00	5.00
	Average	39.22	48.80	NA	15.22	7.20	5.00
	Quantity	6	5	0	9	5	1.00
1"	High	NA	75.00	NA	55.00	17.00	7.00
	Low	NA	50.00	NA	11.00	8.00	5.00
	Average	NA	60.83	NA	28.00	9.08	6.00
	Quantity	0	6	0	4	6	2
1-1/4"	High	NA	NA	NA	NA	65.00	NA
	Low	NA	NA	NA	NA	65.00	NA
	Average	NA	NA	NA	NA	65.00	NA
	Quantity	0	0	0	0	1	0
1-1/2"	High	NA	NA	NA	225.00	NA	NA
	Low	NA	NA	NA	71.00	NA	NA
	Average	NA	NA	NA	142.75	NA	NA
	Quantity	0	0	0	4	0	0

#82. Transition, Leighton. 27/32". $300.

#83. Transition, Leighton. 27/32". $150.

Leighton Transitionals

Up to:		9.9-9.7	9.6-9.3	9.2-9.0	8.9-8.5	8.4-8.0	7.9-7.0
5/8"	High	NA	300.00	410.00	NA	NA	NA
	Low	NA	200.00	410.00	NA	NA	NA
	Average	NA	233.33	410.00	NA	NA	NA
	Quantity	0	3	1	0	0	0
3/4"	High	360.00	NA	280.00	120.00	34.00	NA
	Low	25.00	NA	30.00	27.00	34.00	NA
	Average	192.00	NA	150.50	84.50	34.00	NA
	Quantity	5	0	4	6	1	0
7/8"	High	925.00	285.00	250.00	225.00	76.00	35.00
	Low	55.00	32.00	50.00	22.00	23.00	11.00
	Average	185.33	140.75	101.36	102.18	45.25	19.33
	Quantity	15	4	11	17	4	3
1"	High	260.00	NA	300.00	75.00	150.00	15.00
	Low	260.00	NA	150.00	50.00	150.00	8.00
	Average	260.00	NA	221.37	62.50	150.00	12.00
	Quantity	1	0	8	2	1	3
1-1/4"	High	NA	NA	NA	NA	NA	NA
	Low	NA	NA	NA	NA	NA	NA
	Average	NA	NA	NA	NA	NA	NA
	Quantity	0	0	0	0	0	0
1-1/2"	High	NA	NA	NA	NA	NA	150.00
	Low	NA	NA	NA	NA	NA	50.00
	Average	NA	NA	NA	NA	NA	105.83
	Quantity	0	0	0	0	0	6

FOLD PONTIL TRANSITIONAL

Fold pontil transitionals are also rarer than Melted pontils. The pontil is characterized by a tiny finger of glass that is folded over at the cut-off point and partially melted into the marble surface. This pontil is formed by a similar process to the Pinpoint pontil. The glass was a little too cool when it was sheared off into the machine. As a result, the cut-off spot did not completely melt into the marble because the marble cooled too quickly as it was forming.

Fold Pontil Transitionals

Size		Mint	Near Mint		Good	Collectible	
Up to:		9.9-9.7	9.6-9.3	9.2-9.0	8.9-8.5	8.4-8.0	7.9-7.0
5/8"	High	21.00	NA	20.00	NA	NA	NA
	Low	15.00	NA	19.00	NA	NA	NA
	Average	18.00	NA	19.50	NA	NA	NA
	Quantity	2	0	2	0	0	0
3/4"	High	32.00	NA	NA	NA	NA	NA
	Low	10.00	NA	NA	NA	NA	NA
	Average	15.75	NA	NA	NA	NA	NA
	Quantity	4	0	0	0	0	0
7/8"	High	NA	27.00	NA	NA	NA	NA
	Low	NA	20.50	NA	NA	NA	NA
	Average	NA	25.12	NA	NA	NA	NA
	Quantity	0	4	0	0	0	0

CREASE PONTIL TRANSITIONAL

Crease pontil transitionals are fairly common. It is not known who made these marbles. Evidence points to Germany or Japan: Germany, because many have turned up in recent German finds, and also in lots from England with other German marbles; Japan, because some boxes that are labeled "Made in Japan" have been found to contain them. These marbles are characterized by a spidery crease line that runs along the entire bottom of the marble. Again, the mark was formed because the glass was too cool when it was sheared off as it was dripping into the marble-making machinery. These marbles tend to be transparent blue, aqua, green or brown, with bright opaque white swirls in and on them.

Pinch pontil transitionals are also fairly common. Again, it is not known who made these marbles. There has been speculation that they are German, for the same reason discussed above with crease pontil transitionals. However, the color and style are similar to hand-gathered Christensen Agate marbles, leading some collectors to speculate that they are from that company. Until definitive evidence is discovered, the origin remains a mystery.

#84. Transition, Crease Pontil. 1-1/8". $50.

#85. Transition, Crease Pontil. 7/8". $40.

#86. Transition, Pinch Pontil. 11/16". $15.

#87. Transition, Pinch Pontil. 5/8". $7.50.

Crease/Pinch Pontil Transitionals

Size		Mint	Near Mint		Good	Collectible	
		9.9-9.7	9.6-9.3	9.2-9.0	8.9-8.5	8.4-8.0	7.9-7.0
Up to:							
5/8"	High	10.50	4.25	6.00	2.00	NA	NA
	Low	1.00	2.00	3.00	2.00	NA	NA
	Average	3.94	2.80	4.67	2.00	NA	NA
	Quantity	42	14	3	1	0	0
3/4"	High	21.00	10.00	26.00	19.00	NA	NA
	Low	1.00	3.00	1.00	1.00	NA	NA
	Average	7.29	5.25	4.95	4.60	NA	NA
	Quantity	25	4	24	5	0	0
7/8"	High	21.00	NA	NA	NA	NA	NA
	Low	21.00	NA	NA	NA	NA	NA
	Average	21.00	NA	NA	NA	NA	NA
	Quantity	1	0	0	0	0	0
1-1/4"	High	55.00	NA	42.00	NA	NA	NA
	Low	55.00	NA	42.00	NA	NA	NA
	Average	55.00	NA	42.00	NA	NA	NA
	Quantity	1	0	1	0	0	0

M.F. CHRISTENSEN & SON COMPANY

The M.F. Christensen & Son Company operated in Akron, Ohio, from 1904 until 1917. Martin Christensen patented the first marble-making machine. Many M.F. Christensen marbles are transitionals, because the glass was gathered by a punty and dripped by hand over the rotating machine. The machinery rounded the marble. M.F. Christensen machines did not have automatic feed systems. The molten glass had to be hand-fed off a punty into the machinery. Later M.F. Christensen marbles do not have pontils. This is probably due to refinements in the glass temperature and timing, rather than improvements in the machinery. It is not known if the company ever developed automatic feed or shearing mechanisms.

M.F. Christensen marbles are strictly single-stream marbles. They are either single-color opaque or two-color slag or swirl. This is because the glass for a particular batch was all mixed in one furnace pot and not the separate streams used by later manufacturers. Interestingly, there do not appear to be any M.F. Christensen & Son Company marbles that exhibit a distinctive set of three colors. The company seems to have confined itself to marbles of only one or two color.

OPAQUE

The M.F. Christensen & Son Company produced some opaque marbles. These appear to have been made in limited quantity. Some of these are transitionals. A close examination of M.F. Christensen opaque marbles reveals a faint "9" on the top pole. Generally, you can find them in green ("Imperial Jade"), light blue ("Persion Turquoise"), and yellow. It has been reported that there were some lavender opaques produced, but we have never seen any. We have been approached by many collectors who thought that they had M.F. Christensen opaques, when the marbles were really common game marbles. In fact, these marbles are very, very rare and it is very difficult to assign a value to them.

#88. M.F. Christensen & Son Company, Opaque. 23/32". $150.

#89. M.F. Christensen & Son Company, Opaque. 3/4". $110.

M.F. Christensen & Son Company Opaques

Up to: 5/8"		9.9-9.7	9.6-9.3	9.2-9.0	8.9-8.5	8.4-8.0	7.9-7.0
	High	105.00	NA	NA	50.00	NA	NA
	Low	105.00	NA	NA	27.00	NA	NA
	Average	105.00	NA	NA	36.75	NA	NA
	Quantity	1	0	0	4	0	0
3/4"	High	170.00	NA	190.00	85.00	NA	NA
	Low	170.00	NA	100.00	8.00	NA	NA
	Average	170.00	NA	133.33	37.16	NA	NA
	Quantity	1	0	3	6	0	0

SLAG

The most common M.F. Christensen & Son Company marbles are slags. These marbles have a swirling pattern of transparent colored base with opaque white swirls. M.F. Christensen & Son Company slags are easily identified by the "9" pattern on the top pole and the "cut-off line" on the bottom. These patterns are caused by the twisting motion used in hand gathering the glass out of the furnace and keeping the glass on the end of the punty as a stream of it was allowed to drip into the machine. The marbles are found in blue, green, brown, purple, red, orange, aqua, yellow, and clear. M.F. Christensen slags are found in a wide array of shades of each of the colors mentioned. The brown and purple colors are the most common, perhaps they were the easiest or cheapest to make. The blue and green are next most common, and are fairly easy to find. Clear and aqua are more difficult. Occasionally, the aqua marbles will have a little bit of oxblood in them. Yellow is the second hardest to find and "true" orange is the most difficult color to find. Generally, the better defined the "9", the more valuable the marble. Also, the brighter and clearer the base transparent color, the more highly valued is the marble. Some of these marbles are truly beautiful. The value for slags varies greatly depending on the craftsmanship exhibited in the "9" and the rarity of the hue of the color. There is a wide variation in hues, even within one color, of M.F. Christensen slags. This variation is much more pronounced than you see in other manufacturers. It is not known if this was intentional, or the result of the company's inability to accurately replicate color formulas.

M.F. Christensen & Son Company also made a type of slag that is different than the others. This slag is referred to today as the oxblood slag, although it has been reported that the company named them "moss agate." In reality, the marble looks more like bloodstone than moss agate. The marble is a very dark transparent green base glass with a swirl of oxblood in and on it. Usually, the oxblood forms a "9" and has a tail on the other end. These marbles are often overlooked as just dark opaque game marbles because the base glass is so dark and the oxblood does not really stand out. However, closer examination reveals the oxblood. These marbles are fairly rare.

#90. M.F. Christensen & Son Company, Slag. 1-1/8". $185.

#91. M.F. Christensen & Son Company, Slag. 7/8". $75.

#92. M.F. Christensen & Son Company, Slag. 15/16". $90.

M.F. Christensen & Son Company Slags

Up to:		9.9-9.7	9.6-9.3	9.2-9.0	8.9-8.5	8.4-8.0	7.9-7.0
5/8"	High	140.00	35.00	15.00	3.75	NA	NA
	Low	5.00	6.00	3.00	2.00	NA	NA
	Average	19.34	17.67	9.50	2.71	NA	NA
	Quantity	15	3	8	6	0	0
3/4"	High	23.00	12.00	20.50	7.00	NA	NA
	Low	3.00	2.00	5.00	1.00	NA	NA
	Average	12.15	7.00	11.19	3.80	NA	NA
	Quantity	13	2	8	5	0	0
7/8"	High	65.00	25.00	19.00	11.00	NA	NA
	Low	13.00	25.00	6.00	2.50	NA	NA
	Average	27.95	25.00	13.16	7.38	NA	NA
	Quantity	11	1	6	4	0	0
1"	High	65.00	15.00	17.00	17.00	12.00	9.50
	Low	65.00	15.00	17.00	3.00	6.00	1.00
	Average	65.00	15.00	17.00	10.00	9.00	5.25
	Quantity	1	1	1	2	2	2
1-1/4"	High	NA	NA	NA	NA	NA	NA
	Low	NA	NA	NA	NA	NA	NA
	Average	NA	NA	NA	NA	NA	NA
	Quantity	0	0	0	0	0	0
1-1/2"	High	NA	NA	NA	48.00	31.50	47.00
	Low	NA	NA	NA	48.00	31.50	38.00
	Average	NA	NA	NA	48.00	31.50	42.33
	Quantity	0	0	0	1	1	3

#93. M.F. Christensen & Son Company, Oxblood Slag. 21/32". $250.

M.F. Christensen & Son Company Oxblood Slags

Up to:		9.9-9.7	9.6-9.3	9.2-9.0	8.9-8.5	8.4-8.0	7.9-7.0
5/8"	High	325.00	NA	NA	NA	NA	NA
	Low	210.00	NA	NA	NA	NA	NA
	Average	267.50	NA	NA	NA	NA	NA
	Quantity	2	0	0	0	0	0
3/4"	High	NA	NA	NA	110.00	NA	NA
	Low	NA	NA	NA	110.00	NA	NA
	Average	NA	NA	NA	110.00	NA	NA
	Quantity	0	0	0	1	0	0

BRICK

The most popular M.F. Christensen & Son Company marble is the Brick. It was called the "American Cornelian" by the company. The marble is a combination of oxblood-red and either opaque white, opaque black or both. The common name for the Brick derives from the fact that the marble looks like a piece of brick when it is scuffed up. Each marble is unique in its coloring and pattern. The oxblood-red with black are a little rarer than the oxblood-red with white. There are also a few that have been found that are oxblood-red with dark transparent green. These are really just "oxblood slags" that have mostly oxblood-red and not green. The most highly sought after examples have very well-defined "9"s and tails. Akro Agate Company also made a Brick marble. The Akro bricks tend to be more "purple" and less "oxblood" than the M.F. Christensen Bricks.

#94. M.F. Christensen & Son Company, Brick. 3/4". $90.

#95. M.F. Christensen & Son Company, Brick. 3/4". $75.

M.F. Christensen & Son Company Bricks

Up to: 5/8"		9.9-9.7	9.6-9.3	9.2-9.0	8.9-8.5	8.4-8.0	7.9-7.0
	High	60.00	74.00	40.00	36.00	27.00	13.00
	Low	60.00	55.00	40.00	7.00	11.00	13.00
	Average	60.00	65.50	40.00	24.38	16.75	13.00
	Quantity	1	2	1	8	4	1
3/4"	High	140.00	90.00	100.00	112.50	NA	15.00
	Low	55.00	62.00	32.00	13.00	NA	15.00
	Average	115.67	83.00	70.50	46.28	NA	15.00
	Quantity	3	4	8	9	0	1
7/8"	High	225.00	140.00	210.00	60.00	25.00	25.00
	Low	150.00	73.00	60.00	30.00	22.00	25.00
	Average	175.00	93.25	85.00	45.40	23.50	25.00
	Quantity	3	4	14	5	2	1

CHRISTENSEN AGATE COMPANY

The Christensen Agate Company was founded in 1925 in Payne, Ohio. In 1927, the company moved to Cambridge, Ohio, and was located in a small building near the Cambridge Glass Company. The company had no connection with Martin Christensen or the M.F. Christensen & Son Company. However, the original incorporators may have felt that the use of the Christensen name was a good marketing move.

Christensen Agate produced a variety of marble styles. These marbles were distributed by the company itself, through the J.E. Albright Company of Ravenna, Ohio, and through the Gropper Company of New York City.

The Christensen Agate Company produced only single-stream marbles. They produced all types of single-stream marbles: single-color, slag, and swirl. It does not appear that any Christensen Agate marbles are variegated stream. Many Christensen Agate marbles are made with very brightly colored glass. These are referred to as "electric" colors. The glass colors are unique to Christensen Agate marbles and command much higher prices than the normal colors. Christensen Agate marbles can exhibit either two seams (on opposite sides of the marble), a single seam (e.g., a diaper fold) or no seam. There is very little known about the techniques the company actually used to produce marbles, so it is unclear if different machinery produced each type of marble.

SLAG

Christensen Agate produced slags in a variety of colors. These are transparent color base marbles with opaque white swirls in them. The pattern must be a transparent color base with opaque white. If the marble is two opaque colors, then it is considered a swirl. Also, the opaque white should be randomly swirled through the marble and the surface. If the white is banded or striped on the surface, with only a little inside, it is probably a striped transparent. Generally, the colors of Christensen Agate slags are much brighter than those produced by other manufacturers. Some of the slags have an "electric" color base, usually orange or yellow, which is rarer than the non-"electric" colors. The rarest color is peach, which was not made by any other company.

#96. Christensen Agate Company, Slag. 19/32". $450.

#97. Christensen Agate Company, Slag. 19/32". $75.

Christensen Agate Company Slags

Up to:		9.9-9.7	9.6-9.3	9.2-9.0	8.9-8.5	8.4-8.0	7.9-7.0
1/2"	High	210.00	39.00	43.00	NA	55.00	NA
	Low	19.00	39.00	15.55	NA	4.00	NA
	Average	60.18	39.00	31.64	NA	22.33	NA
	Quantity	27	1	4	0	3	0
5/8"	High	135.00	65.00	55.00	75.00	34.50	7.00
	Low	8.00	16.00	9.00	3.00	6.25	5.00
	Average	30.31	28.33	27.24	18.42	15.76	6.40
	Quantity	46	9	23	17	3	5
3/4"	High	285.00	NA	85.00	23.00	NA	NA
	Low	47.00	NA	9.00	23.00	NA	NA
	Average	172.33	NA	47.00	23.00	NA	NA
	Quantity	3	0	2	1	0	0
7/8"	High	370.00	NA	NA	42.00	90.00	NA
	Low	285.00	NA	NA	7.00	90.00	NA
	Average	327.50	NA	NA	31.75	90.00	NA
	Quantity	2	0	0	4	1	0
1"	High	350.00	NA	NA	100.00	72.00	NA
	Low	350.00	NA	NA	38.00	72.00	NA
	Average	350.00	NA	NA	69.50	72.00	NA
	Quantity	1	0	0	4	1	0

SWIRL

The most common Christensen Agate Company marbles are Swirls. Christensen Agate produced swirls in a great variety of different patterns and color combinations. The marbles were made by mixing two or more glass colors in a single furnace. Because each color was a different density, they did not melt together, but rather created strata. Since the molten glass was the consistency of molasses, the individual stratum remained as the glass was turned into marbles. There are an almost endless variety of colors and patterns in Christensen Agate swirls. Most swirls are in the 9/16" to 3/4" range. Peewees are slightly rarer and marbles over 3/4" are very rare.

White based swirls are the most common, but there are also many examples of swirls with no white in them. The marbles can be two-color or multiple colors. There do not seem to be any swirls with more than five colors in them. Generally, each color is opaque, although there are some marbles that have at least one transparent color. The colors can also be dull, or very bright. Bright colors are referred to as "electric."

Occasionally, the swirl patterns form a row, or two opposing rows, that look like the flames that were painted on the sides of hot rods during the 1950s. Marbles with these patterns are called Flames by collectors today and are rare.

Another rare type of swirl is the transparent swirl. These have a transparent base with another color swirled in. The second color can be opaque, translucent or transparent. That color is usually electric. Clear is the most common base color, with some green, yellow or blue examples known. The most common swirl colors are yellow and orange. Lavender has also been seen. These marbles are fairly rare.

#98. Christensen Agate Company, Swirl. 5/8". $30.

#99. Christensen Agate Company, Swirl. 21/32". $40.

#100. Christensen Agate Company, Swirl. 5/8". $75.

Christensen Agate Company Swirls

Up to: 1/2"		9.9-9.7	9.6-9.3	9.2-9.0	8.9-8.5	8.4-8.0	7.9-7.0
	High	260.00	31.00	100.00	27.00	6.00	NA
	Low	12.00	19.00	5.00	11.00	6.00	NA
	Average	60.34	23.00	26.76	17.17	6.00	NA
	Quantity	21	3	10	3	1	0

5/8"	High	300.00	65.00	95.00	35.00	17.00	NA
	Low	8.00	12.00	5.00	2.00	3.00	NA
	Average	33.04	26.69	18.13	10.49	9.20	NA
	Quantity	278	33	56	31	5	0
3/4"	High	185.00	190.00	80.00	15.00	NA	15.00
	Low	18.00	17.00	8.00	3.00	NA	15.00
	Average	44.82	53.14	29.83	8.51	NA	15.00
	Quantity	11	7	12	5	0	1
7/8"	High	125.00	NA	NA	NA	25.00	NA
	Low	60.00	NA	NA	NA	25.00	NA
	Average	92.50	NA	NA	NA	25.00	NA
	Quantity	2	0	0	0	1	0

STRIPED OPAQUE/
STRIPED TRANSPARENT

Christensen Agate Company also produced a marble similar to the swirls. These were an opaque base with a series of color bands on the surface of one side of the marble, and little or no color on the other side or inside. Usually, the band colors are "electric" and the base can be either opaque or transparent. These are referred to as Striped Opaques and Striped Transparents.

#101. Christensen Agate Company, Striped Opaque. 21/32". $30.

#102. Christensen Agate Company, Striped Opaque. 21/32". $180.

Christensen Agate
Company Striped Opaques

Up to:		9.9-9.7	9.6-9.3	9.2-9.0	8.9-8.5	8.4-8.0	7.9-7.0
1/2"	High	160.00	120.00	15.00	NA	15.00	NA
	Low	33.00	120.00	15.00	NA	15.00	NA
	Average	91.63	120.00	15.00	NA	15.00	NA
	Quantity	12	1	1	0	1	0

5/8"	High	410.00	100.00	175.00	160.00	27.00	NA
	Low	19.00	17.00	10.00	4.00	4.00	NA
	Average	99.60	59.33	48.44	23.11	13.31	NA
	Quantity	54	9	9	15	8	0
3/4"	High	413.00	NA	85.00	NA	NA	NA
	Low	150.00	NA	85.00	NA	NA	NA
	Average	218.50	NA	85.00	NA	NA	NA
	Quantity	2	0	1	0	0	0

Christensen Agate Company Striped Transparents

Up to: 5/8"		9.9-9.7	9.6-9.3	9.2-9.0	8.9-8.5	8.4-8.0	7.9-7.0
	High	400.00	NA	110.00	67.00	50.00	NA
	Low	27.00	NA	110.00	33.00	50.00	NA
	Average	153.64	NA	110.00	50.00	50.00	NA
	Quantity	7	0	1	2	1	0

GUINEA AND COBRA

The "World's Best Guineas" are transparent based marbles with colored flecks of glass melted and stretched on the surface. Occasionally, you will see these flecks inside the marble, particularly in seamed examples. We have been told that the name Guinea originated because the marble colors looked like the heads of the Guinea Cocks that ran around the factory yard. The most common base color is clear, followed by cobalt and then amber. Some green-based Guineas have surfaced, but these are very rare. I have also been told of a couple of red-based Guineas that exist, but have never seen them. The value of a Guinea is also affected by the number of colors on the surface and the intricacy of the pattern. Cobras (sometimes called Cyclones) look like Guineas with all the stretched flecks of colored glass inside the marble. They have only been found in clear base and transparent blue. There are also Guineas with color inside the marble, as well as outside the marble. These are called "Guinea Cobras".

#103. Christensen Agate Company, Guinea. 19/32". $300.

#104. Christensen Agate Company, Guinea. 21/32". $450.

#105. Christensen Agate Company, Guinea/Cobra. 21/32". $650.

#106. Christensen Agate Company, Cobra. 19/32". $700.

Christensen Agate Company Guineas

Up to:		9.9-9.7	9.6-9.3	9.2-9.0	8.9-8.5	8.4-8.0	7.9-7.0
1/2"	High	810.00	NA	NA	NA	NA	NA
	Low	810.00	NA	NA	NA	NA	NA
	Average	810.00	NA	NA	NA	NA	NA
	Quantity	1	0	0	0	0	0
11/16"	High	675.00	330.00	350.00	250.00	NA	90.00
	Low	225.00	260.00	210.00	188.50	NA	75.00
	Average	325.25	298.50	279.44	229.50	NA	82.50
	Quantity	42	10	3	3	0	2

AMERICAN AGATE

An American Agate is a slag type marble of red and white. The red can range from almost a ruddy orange to a bright electric red. The white can be dull or bright. The colors range from translucent to opaque. Some are hand-gathered.

#107. Christensen Agate Company, American Agate. 5/8". $50.

#108. Christensen Agate Company, American Agate. 21/32". $100.

Christensen Agate Company American Agates

Up to:		9.9-9.7	9.6-9.3	9.2-9.0	8.9-8.5	8.4-8.0	7.9-7.9
5/8"	High	50.00	30.00	32.00	17.00	NA	NA
	Low	12.00	30.00	32.00	17.00	NA	NA
	Average	36.00	30.00	32.00	17.00	NA	NA
	Quantity	4	1	4	1	0	0

3/4"							
	High	225.00	NA	55.00	NA	NA	NA
	Low	55.00	NA	55.00	NA	NA	NA
	Average	150.00	NA	55.00	NA	NA	NA
	Quantity	5	0	1	0	0	0

BLOODIE

A Bloodie is a swirl that consists of opaque white, transparent red, and translucent brown. This was a name used by the company.

#109. Christensen Agate Company, Bloodie. 5/8". $60.

Christensen Agate Company Bloodie

Up to: 5/8"		9.9-9.7	9.6-9.3	9.2-9.0	8.9-8.5	8.4-8.0	7.9-7.9
	High	65.00	NA	27.00	25.00	NA	NA
	Low	22.00	NA	27.00	5.00	NA	NA
	Average	46.60	NA	27.00	13.33	NA	NA
	Quantity	5	0	1	3	0	0

EXOTIC

Exotics are a category of Christensen Agate Company marble that has become popular in the past few years. They can be swirls or striped marbles. They have bright electric colors in a non-electric base.

#110. Christensen Agate Company, Exotic. 11/16". $700.

#111. Christensen Agate Company, Exotic. 5/8". $300.

#112. Christensen Agate Company, Exotic. 11/16". $600.

#113. Christensen Agate Company, Exotic. 5/8". $1000.

73

Christensen Agate Company Exotic

Up to: 5/8"	9.9-9.7	9.6-9.3	9.2-9.0	8.9-8.5	8.4-8.0	7.9-7.9
High	750.00	310.00	NA	NA	NA	NA
Low	265.00	310.00	NA	NA	NA	NA
Average	485.00	310.00	NA	NA	NA	NA
Quantity	7	1	0	0	0	0

FLAME SWIRL

A Flame Swirl is a type of swirl that has a flame-like pattern on it, similar to the flames painted on hot rods.

#114. Christensen Agate Company, Flame Swirl. 5/8". $300.

#115. Christensen Agate Company, Flame Swirl. 5/8". $200.

#116. Christensen Agate Company, Flame Swirl. 5/8". $100.

Christensen Agate Company Flame Swirl

Up to:	9.9-9.7	9.6-9.3	9.2-9.0	8.9-8.5	8.4-8.0	7.9-7.9
5/8" High	435.00	350.00	385.00	135.00	61.00	16.00
Low	75.00	350.00	37.00	32.00	12.00	11.00
Average	219.66	350.00	119.60	81.00	37.68	13.50
Quantity	18	1	24	7	3	2
3/4" High	750.00	NA	225.00	385.00	NA	NA
Low	750.00	NA	225.00	385.00	NA	NA
Average	750.00	NA	225.00	385.00	NA	NA
Quantity	1	0	1	1	0	0

HANDGATHERED

Handgathered marbles are the earliest produced by Christensen Agate Company. They were all likely produced in Payne Ohio between 1925 and 1927. The marbles are opaque two-color and are very difficult to find.

#117. Christensen Agate
Company, Handgathered.
5/8". $300.

#118. Christensen Agate
Company, Handgathered.
21/32". $300.

Christensen Agate Company Handgathered

Up to: 5/8"		9.9-9.7	9.6-9.3	9.2-9.0	8.9-8.5	8.4-8.0	7.9-7.9
	High	450.00	225.00	NA	175.00	NA	NA
	Low	160.00	225.00	NA	40.00	NA	NA
	Average	303.33	225.00	NA	107.50	NA	NA
	Quantity	3	1	0	2	0	0

AKRO AGATE COMPANY

The Akro Agate Company was formed in 1910 in Akron, Ohio. It was moved to Clarksburg, West Virginia, in 1914, where it remained until its bankruptcy in 1951. The company originally repackaged marbles bought from the M.F. Christensen and Son Company. By the time the company had moved to Clarksburg, it was operating its own marble making machinery and producing marbles.

Throughout most of the history of the company, Akro Agate was the largest manufacturer of marbles in the United States. The company introduced a number of improvements and design changes to its machinery, which yielded several different types of marbles that could not be replicated by competitors. Many Akro Agate marbles are very collectible today.

The company produced both single-stream and variegated stream marbles, in all types except ribboned and veneered.

OPAQUE

As with many of the other manufacturers of the time, Akro Agate produced a staggering number of single-color marbles. They produced both clearies, which are transparent clear or transparent colored glass marbles, and opaques, which are opaque colored glass marbles. These marbles have little value to today's collectors for several reasons. First, they were produced in such mass quantity that they are abundantly available. Second, since they were the easiest marble to produce, every marble company produced them. It is virtually impossible to distinguish between each company's marbles of this type. Finally, because the marbles are only one color, they do not have much eye appeal.

The exception to this are a series of opaques that were produced with opalescent glass. Opaque marbles of white opalescent glass were called Flint Moonies by the company and are referred to today as Moonies. Opaque marbles of colored opalescent glass are referred to collectively as Flinties. Brown is the most common, followed by yellow, green, red, and blue. These marbles are actually semi-opaque and have a distinctive orangish glow when held to a light. The Moonies are relatively easy to find. The Flinties are more difficult. It appears that Flinties were not produced in as great quantities as Moonies and these marbles are often mistaken for game marbles by collectors. Flinties can be found in many No. 150 and No. 200 tins.

#119. Akro Agate
Company, Moonie. 11/16". $20.

Akro Agate Company Moonie

Up to:		9.9-9.7	9.6-9.3	9.2-9.0	8.9-8.5	8.4-8.0	7.9-7.9
5/8"	High	30.00	NA	NA	1.00	NA	NA
	Low	8.00	NA	NA	1.00	NA	NA
	Average	16.00	NA	NA	1.00	NA	NA
	Quantity	6	0	0	1	0	0
3/4"	High	31.00	NA	NA	29.00	NA	NA
	Low	10.00	NA	NA	7.00	NA	NA
	Average	16.80	NA	NA	14.67	NA	NA
	Quantity	5	0	0	3	0	0

#120. Akro Agate Company, Flintie. 19/32". $15.

#121. Akro Agate Company, Flintie. 5/8". $15.

Akro Agate
Company Flintie

Up to:		9.9-9.7	9.6-9.3	9.2-9.0	8.9-8.5	8.4-8.0	7.9-7.9
5/8"	High	40.00	19.00	19.00	NA	NA	NA
	Low	15.00	19.00	10.00	NA	NA	NA
	Average	24.80	19.00	15.19	NA	NA	NA
	Quantity	5	1	5	0	0	0
3/4"	High	25.00	NA	15.00	10.00	NA	NA
	Low	25.00	NA	15.00	8.00	NA	NA
	Average	25.00	NA	15.00	9.00	NA	NA
	Quantity	1	0	1	2	0	0

SLAG

The other single-stream marble that Akro Agate produced was the slag. Akro Agate produced a large quantity of slags. It would be a fair statement that there are more Akro Agate slags available than those of the three other slag manufacturers (M.F. Christensen, Christensen Agate, and Peltier) combined. The most common color is amber, followed by purple, blue, green, red, aqua, clear, yellow, and orange.

#122. Akro Agate Company, Slag. 5/8" to 11/16". $2 to 10 each.

#123. Akro Agate Company, Slag. 21/32". $15.

#124. Akro Agate Company, Slag. 21/32". $10.

Akro Agate
Company Slags

Up to:		9.9-9.7	9.6-9.3	9.2-9.0	8.9-8.5	8.4-8.0	7.9-7.0
5/8"	High	49.99	28.00	17.00	14.00	2.00	NA
	Low	0.50	1.00	0.50	0.25	1.00	NA
	Average	8.35	6.53	4.04	4.23	1.50	NA
	Quantity	177	28	52	33	2	0
3/4"	High	140.00	26.00	47.00	15.00	5.00	3.00
	Low	3.00	3.00	0.50	0.25	2.00	3.00
	Average	20.02	11.73	9.97	4.46	3.50	3.00
	Quantity	84	13	42	25	2	1
7/8"	High	37.00	35.00	15.00	61.00	9.00	2.00
	Low	17.00	9.00	6.00	4.00	1.00	2.00
	Average	28.43	20.66	11.00	12.88	5.04	2.00
	Quantity	7	6	6	20	13	2
1"	High	76.00	NA	30.00	29.00	NA	8.00
	Low	76.00	NA	30.00	28.00	NA	8.00
	Average	76.00	NA	30.00	28.50	NA	8.00
	Quantity	1	0	1	2	0	1
1-1/4"	High	110.00	NA	85.00	26.00	15.50	40.00
	Low	110.00	NA	30.00	14.00	13.00	3.00
	Average	110.00	NA	54.00	20.00	14.25	16.25
	Quantity	1	0	3	2	2	8

CORNELIAN

A Cornelian is very similar to a Brick, except it is not oxblood. The base is opaque to semi-opaque red, with white swirls in it.

#125. Akro Agate Company,
Cornelian. 5/8". $40.

Cornelian

Up to:		9.9-9.7	9.6-9.3	9.2-9.0	8.9-8.5	8.4-8.0	7.9-7.0
5/8"	High	45.00	40.00	NA	NA	NA	
	Low	12.00	10.00	NA	NA	NA	
	Average	22.50	17.66	NA	NA	NA	
	Quantity	5	6	0	0	0	
3/4"	High	48.00	NA	24.00	13.00	NA	NA
	Low	17.00	NA	15.00	13.00	NA	NA
	Average	29.67	NA	18.00	13.00	NA	NA
	Quantity	3	0	5	1	0	0

OXBLOOD

Akro Agate produced several different types of variegated-stream swirls. Some of these swirls that are collectible today were produced in the same colors as the corkscrew "Ades" (discussed below). However, the most collectible are the oxbloods. Oxblood actually refers to a specific color that is found on the marble. This is a deep rust red with black filaments in it. The color is very similar to dried blood, hence the name. It is often confused with red colors of other manufacturers. However, those colors are almost always translucent to transparent and do not have black filaments. Oxblood must be opaque and it must have black filaments in it.

Oxbloods are found in corkscrew, swirl or patch varieties. They are usually referred to by the name of the underlying marble that they are found on: Chocolate oxblood (opaque brown or dark tan base with oxblood), clear oxblood (transparent clear base with oxblood), milky oxblood (translucent white base with oxblood), silver oxblood (translucent silver base with opaque white swirls and oxblood), limeade oxblood (limeade corkscrew with oxblood), egg yolk oxblood (milky white base with a bright yellow swirl and oxblood), Carnelian oxblood (Carnelian Agate with oxblood), blue oxblood (milky white base with a translucent blue swirl and oxblood), orange oxblood (milky white base with translucent orange swirls and oxblood), lemonade oxblood (milky white base with yellow swirl and oxblood), oxblood corkscrew (opaque white base with an oxblood corkscrew, sometimes on a dark blue spiral, which is called a blue-blood), swirl oxblood (white base with oxblood swirls), patch oxblood (white base with a stripe of oxblood on one side). The swirl and patch oxbloods are generally believed to be more recent than the others. Also, some hybrid examples, which are combinations of two of the above, have been found, but they are extremely rare. Generally, the oxblood floats on the surface of the marble. It is less common to find some of the oxblood inside the marble.

#126. Akro Agate Company, Blue Oxblood. 11/16". $75.

#127. Akro Agate Company, Blue Oxblood. 11/16". $75.

79

Akro Agate Company
Blue Oxblood

Up to:		9.9-9.7	9.6-9.3	9.2-9.0	8.9-8.5	8.4-8.0	7.9-7.9
5/8"	High	85.00	NA	NA	55.00	36.00	NA
	Low	49.00	NA	NA	15.00	15.00	NA
	Average	71.00	NA	NA	32.17	25.50	NA
	Quantity	4	0	0	6	2	0
3/4"	High	190.00	140.00	150.00	80.00	37.00	NA
	Low	64.00	85.00	150.00	37.00	17.00	NA
	Average	114.83	111.67	150.00	55.67	27.00	NA
	Quantity	6	3	1	3	2	0

#128. Akro Agate Company, Carnelian Oxblood. 11/16". $75.

#129. Akro Agate Company, Carnelian Oxblood. 11/16". $60.

Akro Agate Company
Carnelian Oxblood

Up to:		9.9-9.7	9.6-9.3	9.2-9.0	8.9-8.5	8.4-8.0	7.9-7.9
5/8"	High	80.00	NA	65.00	NA	NA	NA
	Low	80.00	NA	20.00	NA	NA	NA
	Average	80.00	NA	42.50	NA	NA	NA
	Quantity	1	0	2	0	0	0
3/4"	High	NA	NA	160.00	33.00	NA	NA
	Low	NA	NA	65.00	25.00	NA	NA
	Average	NA	NA	112.50	29.00	NA	NA
	Quantity	0	0	2	2	0	0

#130. Akro Agate
Company, Egg Yolk
Oxblood. 11/16". $75.

#131. Akro Agate
Company, Egg Yolk
Oxblood. 11/16". $75.

Akro Agate Company Egg Yolk Oxblood

Up to:		9.9-9.7	9.6-9.3	9.2-9.0	8.9-8.5	8.4-8.0	7.9-7.9
5/8"	High	135.00	110.00	135.00	55.00	NA	NA
	Low	76.00	110.00	55.00	26.00	NA	NA
	Average	98.71	110.00	88.75	38.00	NA	NA
	Quantity	7	1	4	3	0	0
3/4"	High	180.00	NA	61.00	90.00	48.00	NA
	Low	100.00	NA	50.00	38.00	48.00	NA
	Average	140.00	NA	55.50	58.60	48.00	NA
	Quantity	2	0	2	5	1	0

#132. Akro Agate
Company, Lemon-
ade Oxblood.
21/32". $45.

#133. Akro Agate
Company,
Lemonade
Oxblood. 21/32".
$45.

Akro Agate Company Lemonade Oxblood

Up to:		9.9-9.7	9.6-9.3	9.2-9.0	8.9-8.5	8.4-8.0	7.9-7.9
5/8"	High	70.00	55.00	55.00	36.00	6.00	NA
	Low	34.00	33.00	30.00	17.00	6.00	NA
	Average	53.29	43.00	41.89	25.14	6.00	NA
	Quantity	14	4	9	7	1	0
3/4"	High	290.00	NA	160.00	125.00	NA	12.00
	Low	95.00	NA	75.00	36.00	NA	12.00
	Average	199.00	NA	117.50	65.71	NA	12.00
	Quantity	5	0	2	7	0	1

#134. Akro Agate
Company, Limeade
Oxblood. 5/8". $155.

#135. Akro Agate
Company, Limeade
Oxblood. 5/8". $125.

Akro Agate Company
Limeade Oxblood

Up to: 5/8"		9.9-9.7	9.6-9.3	9.2-9.0	8.9-8.5	8.4-8.0	7.9-7.9
	High	260.00	NA	235.00	150.00	36.00	NA
	Low	50.00	NA	235.00	42.00	23.00	NA
	Average	130.00	NA	235.00	79.25	28.00	NA
	Quantity	7	0	1	4	3	0

#136. Akro Agate
Company, Milky
Oxblood. 11/16". $40.

#137. Akro Agate
Company, Milky
Oxblood. 21/32". $35.

Akro Agate Company
Milky Oxblood

Up to:		9.9-9.7	9.6-9.3	9.2-9.0	8.9-8.5	8.4-8.0	7.9-7.9
5/8"	High	55.00	NA	15.00	19.00	NA	NA
	Low	13.00	NA	12.00	5.00	NA	NA
	Average	30.52	NA	13.50	10.67	NA	NA
	Quantity	9	0	2	3	0	0
3/4"	High	125.00	NA	95.00	NA	NA	NA
	Low	55.00	NA	37.00	NA	NA	NA
	Average	78.75	NA	59.00	NA	NA	NA
	Quantity	4	0	3	0	0	0

#138. Akro Agate Company, Oxblood Corkscrew. 21/32". $75.

#139. Akro Agate Company, Oxblood Corkscrew. 5/8". $60.

Akro Agate Company
Oxblood Corkscrew

Up to:		9.9-9.7	9.6-9.3	9.2-9.0	8.9-8.5	8.4-8.0	7.9-7.9
5/8"	High	130.00	NA	NA	80.00	NA	NA
	Low	50.00	NA	NA	13.00	NA	NA
	Average	95.00	NA	NA	29.38	NA	NA
	Quantity	5	0	0	13	0	0
3/4"	High	NA	NA	NA	70.00	NA	NA
	Low	NA	NA	NA	50.00	NA	NA
	Average	NA	NA	NA	60.00	NA	NA
	Quantity	0	0	0	4	0	0

#140. Akro Agate Company, Silver Oxblood. 5/8". $40.

#141. Akro Agate Company, Silver Oxblood. 11/16". $40.

Akro Agate Company
Silver Oxblood

Up to:		9.9-9.7	9.6-9.3	9.2-9.0	8.9-8.5	8.4-8.0	7.9-7.9
5/8"	High	70.00	NA	35.00	30.00	12.00	NA
	Low	21.00	NA	19.00	12.00	12.00	NA
	Average	43.61	NA	27.33	17.50	12.00	NA
	Quantity	37	0	6	6	1	0
3/4"	High	135.00	NA	135.00	44.00	NA	NA
	Low	55.00	NA	35.00	9.00	NA	NA
	Average	94.00	NA	85.00	26.00	NA	NA
	Quantity	5	0	2	4	0	0

#142. Akro Agate Company, Swirl Oxblood. 11/16". $15.

#143. Akro Agate Company, Swirl Oxblood. 5/8". $15.

Akro Agate Company
Swirl Oxblood

Up to:		9.9-9.7	9.6-9.3	9.2-9.0	8.9-8.5	8.4-8.0	7.9-7.9
5/8"	High	27.00	18.25	23.00	18.39	NA	NA
	Low	6.00	8.00	4.00	3.00	NA	NA
	Average	14.74	12.59	11.33	8.48	NA	NA
	Quantity	49	8	21	5	0	0

#144. Akro Agate Company, Patch Oxblood. 7/8". $30.

#145. Akro Agate Company, Patch Oxblood. 15/16". $30.

Akro Agate Company
Patch Oxblood

Up to:		9.9-9.7	9.6-9.3	9.2-9.0	8.9-8.5	8.4-8.0	7.9-7.0
5/8"	High	19.00	8.50	9.00	22.00	NA	NA
	Low	1.00	3.00	1.00	1.00	NA	NA
	Average	5.34	5.50	5.00	10.23	NA	NA
	Quantity	34	7	2	11	0	0
3/4"	High	8.00	NA	11.00	NA	NA	NA
	Low	8.00	NA	5.00	NA	NA	NA
	Average	8.00	NA	6.75	NA	NA	NA
	Quantity	1	0	4	0	0	0
7/8"	High	32.00	NA	25.00	4.00	NA	NA
	Low	12.00	NA	7.00	4.00	NA	NA
	Average	19.53	NA	10.49	4.00	NA	NA
	Quantity	14	0	13	1	0	0
1"	High	NA	80.00	65.00	21.00	NA	NA
	Low	NA	80.00	65.00	13.00	NA	NA
	Average	NA	80.00	65.00	17.00	NA	NA
	Quantity	0	1	1	2	0	0

CORKSCREW

The most common and easily recognizable Akro Agate marble is the corkscrew. This is a variegated-stream marble whose design is unique to Akro Agate. Two or more streams of colored glass were allowed to enter through the marble-making machine's shearing mechanism at the same time. Because the different colors were layered as they came out of the furnace and because the colors were of different densities, they created separate strata in the glass stream as it entered the shearing mechanism. Just before the shearing mechanism in the Akro machinery there was a small cup with a hole in the bottom. The glass stream entered the cup from the top and passed through the hole in the bottom into the shearing mechanism. If the cup was spinning, then a corkscrew was created. If the cup was not spinning, then a patch was created. The number of different colored spirals in the corkscrew, or the number of different color patches, was determined by the number of nozzles that had glass flowing through them when the glass stream was created.

Corkscrews are identifiable as being two or more spirals of color that rotate around the marble from one pole to the other, but do not intersect. Different color combinations and designs were marketed by Akro Agate under a variety of names: Prize Name (two opaque colors), Special (three or more opaque colors), Ace (one opaque color and translucent milky white), Spiral (transparent clear base with colored spiral), Onyx (transparent color base with opaque white spiral). In addition, other names have been applied by children and collectors over the years: Snake (a Spiral or Onyx where the opaque or colored glass is on the surface and just below it), Ribbon (a Spiral or Onyx where the opaque or colored glass goes almost to the center of the marble), "Ades" (types of Aces with fluorescent base glass), and Popeye (a specific type of Special commonly found in Popeye marble boxes).

Two-colored white-based Prize Names are the most common corkscrew type. This is followed by two-colored color-based Prize Names, Onyx, Spirals, three-color Specials, Aces, four-color Specials, and five-color Specials. Although I have heard of six color corkscrews, I have never actually seen an example where the sixth color was not actually a blend of two of the other colors.

#147. Akro Agate Company, Corkscrew. 21/32". $15.

#148. Akro Agate Company, Corkscrew. 5/8". $15.

#146. Akro Agate Company, Corkscrew. 21/32". $5.

#149. Akro Agate Company, Corkscrew. 11/16". $40.

Akro Agate Company
Corkscrews

Up to:		9.9-9.7	9.6-9.3	9.2-9.0	8.9-8.5	8.4-8.0	7.9-7.0
5/8"	High	350.00	42.00	65.00	50.00	15.00	3.00
	Low	0.50	1.00	0.50	0.25	0.50	3.00
	Average	14.40	9.41	9.21	5.60	4.75	3.00
	Quantity	808	81	227	148	8	1
3/4"	High	140.00	85.00	110.00	43.00	9.00	NA
	Low	2.00	3.00	2.00	0.50	0.25	NA
	Average	22.58	35.80	16.48	7.44	5.46	NA
	Quantity	70	15	31	33	7	0
7/8"	High	150.00	65.00	140.00	110.00	12.00	3.51
	Low	5.00	6.00	2.00	1.00	9.00	2.00
	Average	30.85	21.83	22.92	11.08	10.50	2.75
	Quantity	28	40	28	51	2	2
1"	High	320.00	30.00	80.00	50.00	2.00	2.00
	Low	21.00	20.00	5.00	2.00	0.25	2.00
	Average	84.53	24.31	24.26	11.77	1.13	2.00
	Quantity	15	13	42	49	2	4
1-1/4"	High	900.00	510.00	325.00	160.00	NA	NA
	Low	900.00	510.00	325.00	160.00	NA	NA
	Average	900.00	510.00	325.00	160.00	NA	NA
	Quantity	1	1	1	1	0	0

POPEYE CORKSCREW

Popeye corkscrews are three-color or four-color Specials that contain a unique color spiral. This unique color is transparent clear with filaments of opaque white. The filaments can almost completely fill the transparent clear or they can be sparse. The most common colors, in addition to the clear/white, are red and yellow or green and yellow. These are followed (in order of increasing rarity) by red and green, dark blue and yellow, light purple and yellow, dark purple and yellow, powder blue and yellow, red and blue, red and orange, blue and green, black and yellow, or various hybrid colors. Hybrid Popeyes are marbles that have three or four colors along with the clear/white. It is popularly believed that these marbles occurred when the colors were changed in one of the machine hoppers. However, some of these examples are too perfectly formed to be an accident. They may have been intentionally made by using five nozzles, instead of four, to create the glass stream. There are some Popeye corkscrews that have a fourth color that is really just a blending of the two colored glass streams. These really are not hybrids. True hybrids are rare and are highly prized by collectors.

Some Popeyes were produced when the spinning cup in the machine was not rotating. As a result, these marbles came out as patches. They are the same color combinations as Popeyes, but are actually two or three distinct patches of color on a clear/white base. These are called Patch Popeyes and are very rare. They have been easily confused with a type of Vitro Agate patch, and have fallen out of favor with collectors at this time.

There are also several types of corkscrews that have the clear/white color combination as Popeyes, but only one other colored spiral (usually translucent red or orange) These are usually referred to as Ringers or Imperials, and are not really Popeyes.

#150. Akro Agate Company, Popeye Corkscrew. 21/32". $20.

#151. Akro Agate Company, Popeye Corkscrew. 5/8". $75.

#152. Akro Agate Company, Popeye Corkscrew. 21/32". $400.

Akro Agate Company
Popeye Corkscrews

Up to:		9.9-9.7	9.6-9.3	9.2-9.0	8.9-8.5	8.4-8.0	7.9-7.9
5/8"	High	124.00	80.00	85.00	60.00	55.00	12.57
	Low	12.01	12.00	8.00	5.00	4.00	8.00
	Average	45.96	31.71	28.89	16.89	14.35	10.39
	Quantity	195	12	58	50	8	4
3/4"	High	360.00	155.00	220.00	135.00	34.00	20.00
	Low	15.00	27.00	12.00	9.00	3.00	11.00
	Average	52.33	85.75	71.35	37.27	13.55	15.50
	Quantity	56	11	44	28	9	3

Analysis by Color of
Popeyes for
Condition 9.9 - 9.3

Up to:		High	Low	Average	Quality
5/8"	Red/Yellow	35.00	12.00	21.12	60
	Green/Yellow				
	Red/Green	33.00	13.00	24.67	43
	Blue/Yellow	43.00	19.00	34.53	57
	Purple/Yellow	112.00	54.00	96.90	22
	Red/Blue	124.00	76.00	115.45	25

ADES

The "Ades" are also a specialized type of corkscrew. Ades contain a corkscrew that consists of a fluorescent milky off-white glass with filaments of opaque white and a spiral of a translucent color. If the color is yellow, then it is called a lemonade, green is called a limeade, orange is called an orangeade, red is called cherry-ade, and brown is called a Carnelian. The Carnelian is the only one that is actually the name used by Akro Agate. Some of these marbles are really swirls, and not distinctive corkscrews. This does not affect the value.

#153. Akro Agate Company, Cherryade. 27/32". $75.

#154. Akro Agate Company, Cherryade. 3/4". $60.

Akro Agate Company
Cherryade

Up to:		9.9-9.7	9.6-9.3	9.2-9.0	8.9-8.5	8.4-8.0	7.9-7.0
5/8"	High	65.00	NA	NA	20.00	NA	NA
	Low	47.00	NA	NA	10.00	NA	NA
	Average	56.45	NA	NA	15.00	NA	NA
	Quantity	6	0	0	2	0	0
3/4"	High	NA	NA	NA	NA	NA	NA
	Low	NA	NA	NA	NA	NA	NA
	Average	NA	NA	NA	NA	NA	NA
	Quantity	0	0	0	0	0	0
7/8"	High	NA	NA	NA	NA	NA	NA
	Low	NA	NA	NA	NA	NA	NA
	Average	NA	NA	NA	NA	NA	NA
	Quantity	0	0	0	0	0	0
1"	High	NA	NA	85.00	90.00	NA	NA
	Low	NA	NA	50.00	25.00	NA	NA
	Average	NA	NA	67.50	42.92	NA	NA
	Quantity	0	0	2	12	0	0

#155. Akro Agate Company, Lemonade. 11/16". $15.

#156. Akro Agate Company, Lemonade. 21/32". $12.5.

Akro Agate Company
Lemonade

Up to: 7.9-7.0		9.9-9.7	9.6-9.3	9.2-9.0	8.9-8.5	8.4-8.0	
5/8"	High	42.00	NA	42.00	30.00	NA	NA
	Low	7.00	NA	5.00	2.00	NA	NA
	Average	16.96	NA	14.14	7.59	NA	NA
	Quantity	23	0	7	13	0	0
3/4"	High	NA	NA	NA	7.00	NA	NA
	Low	NA	NA	NA	7.00	NA	NA
	Average	NA	NA	NA	7.00	NA	NA
	Quantity	0	0	0	1	0	0
7/8"	High	NA	NA	NA	NA	NA	NA
	Low	NA	NA	NA	NA	NA	NA
	Average	NA	NA	NA	NA	NA	NA
	Quantity	0	0	0	0	0	0
1"	High	NA	NA	35.00	37.00	NA	NA
	Low	NA	NA	35.00	2.00	NA	NA
	Average	NA	NA	35.00	22.43	NA	NA
	Quantity	0	0	1	6	0	0

#157. Akro Agate Company, Limeade. 21/32". $20.

#158. Akro Agate Company, Limeade. 11/16". $25.

Akro Agate Company
Limeade

Up to:		9.9-9.7	9.6-9.3	9.2-9.0	8.9-8.5	8.4-8.0	7.9-7.0
5/8"	High	46.00	70.00	32.00	17.00	NA	NA
	Low	14.00	20.00	12.00	3.00	NA	NA
	Average	26.09	38.33	20.25	8.40	NA	NA
	Quantity	17	3	4	5	0	0
3/4"	High	NA	NA	NA	NA	21.00	NA
	Low	NA	NA	NA	NA	8.00	NA
	Average	NA	NA	NA	NA	14.50	NA
	Quantity	0	0	0	0	2	0

		9.9-9.7	9.6-9.3	9.2-9.0	8.9-8.5	8.4-8.0	7.9-7.0
7/8"	High	NA	NA	NA	31.00	NA	NA
	Low	NA	NA	NA	13.00	NA	NA
	Average	NA	NA	NA	22.96	NA	NA
	Quantity	0	0	0	7	0	0
1"	High	NA	NA	NA	47.00	NA	NA
	Low	NA	NA	NA	30.00	NA	NA
	Average	NA	NA	NA	35.50	NA	NA
	Quantity	0	0	0	4	0	0

Akro Agate Company
Orangeade

Up to:		9.9-9.7	9.6-9.3	9.2-9.0	8.9-8.5	8.4-8.0	7.9-7.0
5/8"	High	110.00	NA	55.00	23.50	NA	NA
	Low	55.00	NA	40.00	20.00	NA	NA
	Average	79.86	NA	47.50	21.75	NA	NA
	Quantity	7	0	2	2	0	0

 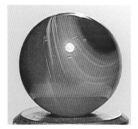

#159. Akro Agate Company, Carnelian. 21/32". $20.

#160. Akro Agate Company, Carnelian. 5/8". $20.

Akro Agate Company
Carnelian

Up to:		9.9-9.7	9.6-9.3	9.2-9.0	8.9-8.5	8.4-8.0	7.9-7.0
5/8"	High	35.56	33.50	29.00	9.57	NA	NA
	Low	15.00	11.00	8.00	6.00	NA	NA
	Average	21.07	19.56	13.20	7.01	NA	NA
	Quantity	8	7	5	8	0	0
3/4"	High	48.00	NA	24.00	13.00	NA	NA
	Low	17.00	NA	15.00	13.00	NA	NA
	Average	29.67	NA	18.00	13.00	NA	NA
	Quantity	3	0	5	1	0	0

PATCHES

Another type of machine-made marble that has several variations which are uniquely Akro Agate are patches. A patch is a corkscrew that was not twisted. It is a variegated stream of glass consisting of two or more colors.

There are several types of patches that Akro Agate marketed under various names, including Hero, Unique, Moss Agate, Royal, and Tricolor Agate. The Hero and Unique are the oldest type of Akro Agate patch. These appear to have been produced for a short period of time during the mid-1920s. Both marbles have an opaque white base with a wispy brown patch brushed on about one-third of the marble. The Unique has a small space in the middle of the patch through which the white base shows. The Hero does not have this space. Both of these are readily identifiable because they have a crimp mark at either pole, which indicates that they were produced before the Early Improvement (see glossary). This would date them to the early to mid-1920s. Moss Agates have a two-color patch. One color is a fluorescent translucent milky brownish/white base. The other color is a translucent colored patch (generally brown, yellow, red, blue or green) that covers one-quarter to almost one-half the marble. An Akro Royal is a two-color patch. The base color is opaque. The patch is either opaque or transparent and usually covers about one-quarter of the marble. A Tricolor Agate is a white base with two differently colored patches on it.

#161. Akro Agate
Company, Moss Agate.
7/8". $10.

Akro Agate Company
Moss Agate

Up to:		9.9-9.7	9.6-9.3	9.2-9.0	8.9-8.5	8.4-8.0	7.9-7.0
5/8"	High	11.00	11.00	15.00	2.00	NA	NA
	Low	1.00	11.00	2.00	2.00	NA	NA
	Average	6.44	11.00	5.75	2.00	NA	NA
	Quantity	29	1	4	1	0	0
3/4"	High	8.00	NA	12.00	NA	NA	NA
	Low	8.00	NA	1.00	NA	NA	NA
	Average	8.00	NA	6.29	NA	NA	NA
	Quantity	1	0	7	0	0	0
7/8"	High	15.00	NA	12.50	NA	NA	NA
	Low	15.00	NA	3.00	NA	NA	NA
	Average	15.00	NA	8.44	NA	NA	NA
	Quantity	1	0	7	0	0	0
1"	High	30.00	NA	17.00	6.00	NA	NA
	Low	30.00	NA	6.00	3.00	NA	NA
	Average	30.00	NA	9.67	4.83	NA	NA
	Quantity	1	0	3	3	0	0

#162. Akro Agate
Company, Royal.
21/32". $2.

#163. Akro Agate Com-
pany, Royal. 21/32". $2.

Akro Agate Company
Royal

Up to: 5/8"		9.9-9.7	9.6-9.3	9.2-9.0	8.9-8.5	8.4-8.0	7.9-7.0
	High	10.50	3.50	4.00	NA	NA	NA
	Low	1.00	1.00	1.00	NA	NA	NA
	Average	5.70	2.15	2.00	NA	NA	NA
	Quantity	5	3	3	0	0	0

#164. Akro Agate Company,
Tri-color Agate. 3/4". $4 each.

#165. Akro Agate Company, Tri-
color Agate. 11/16". $2 each.

Akro Agate Company
Tricolor Agate

Up to:		9.9-9.7	9.6-9.3	9.2-9.0	8.9-8.5	8.4-8.0	7.9-7.0
5/8"	High	2.00	NA	2.00	NA	NA	NA
	Low	2.00	NA	2.00	NA	NA	NA
	Average	2.00	NA	2.00	NA	NA	NA
	Quantity	1	0	1	0	0	0
3/4"	High	15.00	5.00	8.75	NA	NA	NA
	Low	0.50	5.00	8.75	NA	NA	NA
	Average	6.06	5.00	8.75	NA	NA	NA
	Quantity	8	1	1	0	0	0

7/8"	High	17.00	NA	NA	NA	NA	NA
	Low	9.00	NA	NA	NA	NA	NA
	Average	12.33	NA	NA	NA	NA	NA
	Quantity	3	0	0	0	0	0

SPARKLER

Another type of marble that is unique to Akro Agate is the Sparkler. This is a clear base marble with filaments and strands of various colors running inside the marble from pole to pole. It appears to be made using the same technique as some cat's-eyes, in that various colors of glass are injected into a clear stream as it flows through the furnace. However, Sparklers pre-date all other cat's-eyes by at least fifteen years and they seem to pre-date even Peltier Bananas. Sparklers were produced in the mid- to late 1920s and do not appear to have been produced much past 1930. They have generally only been found in the 5/8" to 3/4" size. Sparklers are often confused with clear Master Marble Sunbursts. They can be differentiated by several features. Sparklers tend to have brighter colors than Sunbursts. Also, Sparklers usually have five different colors in them, whereas Sunbursts have at most three different colors. There is also another marble that is very similar to Sparklers and is usually referred to as a "foreign sparkler". These are a transparent clear base with translucent strands of color running through the center. They usually have a tiny crimp mark at one or both poles. These are easily distinguishable from Akro Sparklers because of the translucence of the colors.

#166. Akro Agate Company, Sparkler. 5/8". $45.

#167. Akro Agate Company, Sparkler. 5/8". $45.

Akro Agate Company Sparklers

Up to:		9.9-9.7	9.6-9.3	9.2-9.0	8.9-8.5	8.4-8.0	7.9-7.0
5/8"	High	105.00	48.00	39.00	32.00	15.00	11.00
	Low	17.00	31.00	17.00	11.00	15.00	11.00
	Average	58.52	39.50	28.82	23.50	15.00	11.00
	Quantity	25	2	11	10	1	1

PELTIER GLASS COMPANY

The Peltier Glass Company was founded in 1886 under the name The Novelty Glass Company by Victor Peltier. The name was changed to the Peltier Glass Company in 1919. The company is located in Ottawa, Illinois, and is still in operation, but no longer produces marbles.

Peltier began making marbles sometime during the early 1920s. Their marbles were marketed under their name and also by M. Gropper & Sons. Peltier produced slags, patches, ribbons, and cat's-eyes. Peltier also produced clearies and opaques, but there is no way to identify them as specific to this company.

SLAG

The earliest Peltier marbles are single-stream. They are usually referred to as "Miller" marbles because they were produced using Peltier's first marble machine, designed by an employee named William Miller. Peltier produced single-stream slags and swirls.

Peltier slags are single-stream marbles, as are the slags of other companies. They are a transparent colored base glass with opaque white swirled in. Peltier slags are rarer than those of the other companies. The most common are brown, blue or green. There are also aqua, purple, red, and yellow. The company does not appear to have produced clear slags. Peltier slags are readily identifiable by the very fine feathering pattern produced by the white swirls. This is unique to Peltier. Their slags (as with many Peltier marbles) also tend to have blown out air holes, which you usually do not see in the marbles of the other companies.

#168. Peltier Glass Company, Slag. 11/16". $20.

#169. Peltier Glass Company, Slag. 5/8". $10.

Peltier Glass Company
Slags

Up to:		9.9-9.7	9.6-9.3	9.2-9.0	8.9-8.5	8.4-8.0	7.9-7.0
5/8"	High	30.00	20.00	11.00	9.50	NA	2.00
	Low	5.00	6.00	10.00	2.00	NA	2.00
	Average	12.32	12.00	10.50	5.12	NA	2.00
	Quantity	11	4	2	4	0	1
3/4"	High	30.00	17.00	25.00	6.00	NA	NA
	Low	22.00	15.00	11.00	5.00	NA	NA
	Average	26.00	16.33	13.00	5.50	NA	NA
	Quantity	2	3	11	2	0	0

MILLER SWIRL

Peltier produced several types of single-stream swirls. These are referred to as "Miller Machine" marbles because they were produced on Peltier's first marble machine, which was designed by a man named William Miller. Peltier used another type of machine to produce Rainbos, etc. That machine does not have a name.

An early type of Peltier multi-color swirl was produced by the "Miller machine". It has a transparent colored base with several opaque colors swirled in, it is much rarer than more common multi-colors where the colors are actually ribbons, not swirls. There are several types of multi-color swirls that have similar coloring to tri-color National Line Rainbos. These are also rare.

Peltier Glass Company
"Miller Machine" Swirls

Up to:		9.9-9.7	9.6-9.3	9.2-9.0	8.9-8.5	8.4-8.0	7.9-7.0
3/4"	High	65.00	NA	NA	NA	NA	NA
	Low	65.00	NA	NA	NA	NA	NA
	Average	65.00	NA	NA	NA	NA	NA
	Quantity	1	0	0	0	0	0
7/8"	High	250.00	NA	NA	NA	NA	NA
	Low	160.00	NA	NA	NA	NA	NA
	Average	195.00	NA	NA	NA	NA	NA
	Quantity	4	0	0	0	0	0

PEERLESS PATCH

Peltier produced a patch marble which they marketed as the Peerless. The Peerless patches are very collectible today. The marbles have a two-color patch. They are identifiable by the uniqueness of their shades of color and by their design. Peerless patches are the type of marble that Peltier Picture Marbles (comics) are on. The most common color combination is black patch on white, green patch on mustard yellow, transparent green patch on white, red on white, yellow on aqua, or red on aqua. There are other color combinations, but they are rarer. The rarest patch color is called "pearlized". This is a greenish color that has a satin shimmer or sheen to it. These are very rare. The design of the patch on Peerless patches is unique. The patches of other companies have straight edges. Peltier marbles have patches that have curved or "S" edges. This feature, along with the unique colors, makes Peerless patches easily identifiable.

#170. Peltier Glass Company, Peerless Patch. 5/8". $5 each.

#171. Peltier Glass Company, Peerless Patch. 5/8". $5.

Peltier Glass Company
Peerless Patches

Up to:		9.9-9.7	9.6-9.3	9.2-9.0	8.9-8.5	8.4-8.0	7.9-7.0
5/8"	High	32.00	27.00	22.00	2.00	NA	NA
	Low	2.00	1.00	1.00	2.00	NA	NA
	Average	8.73	7.75	6.53	2.00	NA	NA
	Quantity	27	5	26	1	0	0
3/4"	High	25.00	16.00	25.00	5.01	NA	NA
	Low	2.00	5.00	8.00	0.25	NA	NA
	Average	12.96	10.50	10.33	2.25	NA	NA
	Quantity	14	2	3	5	0	0

PICTURE MARBLE
"COMIC"

One of the most collectible Peltier Glass marbles is the Picture Marble or comic. These are Peltier Peerless patches with a black transfer of one of twelve different King Syndicate comic characters fired on the marble surface. Usually, there is an overglaze of clear glass. The twelve characters (in ascending order of rarity) are Emma, Koko, Bimbo, Andy, Smitty, Annie, Herbie, Sandy, Skeezix, Betty, Moon, and Kayo. There are also comic marbles with a transfer of Tom Mix and with an advertisement for Cotes Master Loaf on them. These are very rare. The transfers are always on 19/32" to 11/16" Peerless Patches. Each character has a specific marble color combination that is most common to that marble. Rarer color combinations are difficult to find and are valued much higher. Also, there has been a Tom Mix marble reported to have a red transfer, and there has also been a black comic transfer on a 7/8" marble. These are extremely rare, and were probably experimental.

#172. Peltier Glass Company, Picture Marble - Comic. 5/8". $75.

#175. Peltier Glass Company, Picture Marble - Comic. 21/32". $40.

#173. Peltier Glass Company, Picture Marble - Comic. 5/8". $275.

#174. Peltier Glass Company, Picture Marble - Comic. 11/16". $65.

Peltier Glass Company
Picture Marbles ("Comics")

Up to:	9.9-9.7	9.6-9.3	9.2-9.0	8.9-8.5	8.4-8.0	7.9-7.0
11/16" High	370.00	280.00	185.00	60.00	NA	NA
Low	32.00	35.00	35.00	14.00	NA	NA
Average	126.01	162.48	78.67	32.67	NA	NA
Quantity	112	23	6	3	0	0

An Analysis by Comic Character for Condition 9.9-9.3:

Character	High	Low	Average	Quantity
Emma				
Koko	68.00	32.00	44.35	39
Bimbo				
Andy				
Smitty Herbie				
Skeezix	125.00	55.00	76.40	34
Annie				
Sandy	160.00	95.00	122.48	23
Betty	325.00	225.00	245.00	12
Moon	325.00	180.00	262.07	16
Kayo	370.00	210.00	326.33	11

NATIONAL LINE RAINBO

The majority of collectible Peltier Glass Company marbles are ribboned type. The most collectible of these are the National Line Rainbo. These marbles are an opaque base color with four to six thin ribbons in the surface. The tri-colors can be distinguished from "Miller Machine" marbles because they have two seams on them, as if they were two halves that were joined together. Also, the ribbons are usually translucent to transparent on the tri-color National Line Rainbos, and opaque on the "Miller Machine" tri-colors.

If the ribbons are all the same color, then the marble is referred to as a two-color National Line Rainbo. The base color can be either opaque white or an opaque color. Some of the color combinations have inspired imaginative names among collectors. Zebras are black ribbon on white base, Blue Zebras are blue ribbon on white base, Bumblebee is black ribbon on yellow base, Blue Bee is blue aventurine on yellow base, Cub Scout is yellow ribbon on blue base, Wasp is black ribbon on red base, Blue Wasp is blue ribbon on red base, Tiger is black ribbon on orange base, Blue Tiger is blue ribbon on orange base. National Line Rainbos with ribbons of two different colors are called Tri-color National Line Rainbos. They have also inspired a series of imaginative names. Ketchup & Mustard is opaque white base with red and yellow ribbons, Christmas Tree is opaque white base with red and green ribbons, Liberty is opaque white base with red and blue ribbons. Gray-Coat is opaque white base with red and gray ribbons. Rebel is an opaque white or yellow base with black and red ribbons. Golden Rebel is opaque yellow base with red and black ribbons, Superman is opaque light blue base with yellow and red ribbons. Flaming Dragon is red and yellow on opaque green base. Blue Galaxy is red and aventurine black on light blue opaque base. Hybrid examples also exist.

#176. Peltier Glass
Company, Bumblebee.
5/8". $50.

#177. Peltier Glass Company,
Bumblebee. 5/8". $50.

Peltier Glass Company
Bumblebee

Up to:		9.9-9.7	9.6-9.3	9.2-9.0	8.9-8.5	8.4-8.0	7.9-7.0
5/8"	High	60.00	45.00	60.00	12.00	10.00	NA
	Low	24.00	25.00	19.50	2.00	7.00	NA
	Average	43.83	35.00	32.42	7.67	8.50	NA
	Quantity	6	7	6	3	2	0
3/4"	High	125.00	75.00	NA	34.33	NA	NA
	Low	125.00	75.00	NA	5.00	NA	NA
	Average	125.00	75.00	NA	17.58	NA	NA
	Quantity	1	1	0	4	0	0

Peltier Glass Company
Chocolate Cow

Up to:		9.9-9.7	9.6-9.3	9.2-9.0	8.9-8.5	8.4-8.0	7.9-7.0
5/8"	High	165.00	NA	NA	85.00	NA	NA
	Low	165.00	NA	NA	85.00	NA	NA
	Average	165.00	NA	NA	85.00	NA	NA
	Quantity	1	0	0	0	0	0

#178. Peltier Glass Company, Christmas Tree. 21/32". $75.

#179. Peltier Glass Company, Christmas Tree. 5/8". $75.

Peltier Glass Company
Christmas Tree

Up to:		9.9-9.7	9.6-9.3	9.2-9.0	8.9-8.5	8.4-8.0	7.9-7.0
5/8"	High	80.00	62.00	50.00	24.00	15.00	NA
	Low	61.00	62.00	50.00	24.00	15.00	NA
	Average	70.50	62.00	50.00	24.00	15.00	NA
	Quantity	2	1	1	1	1	0
3/4"	High	160.00	NA	90.00	35.00	NA	25.00
	Low	75.00	NA	42.00	20.00	NA	12.00
	Average	107.92	NA	66.00	27.50	NA	18.50
	Quantity	12	0	2	2	0	2
7/8"	High	NA	NA	360.00	75.00	NA	NA
	Low	NA	NA	360.00	75.00	NA	NA
	Average	NA	NA	360.00	75.00	NA	NA
	Quantity	0	0	1	1	0	0

#180. Peltier Glass Company, Flaming Dragon. 5/8". $75.

#181. Peltier Glass Company, Flaming Dragon. 21/32". $60.

Peltier Glass Company
Flaming Dragon

Up to:		9.9-9.7	9.6-9.3	9.2-9.0	8.9-8.5	8.4-8.0	7.9-7.0
5/8"	High	NA	NA	NA	26.25	NA	NA
	Low	NA	NA	NA	12.00	NA	NA
	Average	NA	NA	NA	19.13	NA	NA
	Quantity	0	0	0	2	0	0
3/4"	High	130.00	NA	55.00	NA	NA	11.00
	Low	75.00	NA	55.00	NA	NA	11.00
	Average	103.75	NA	55.00	NA	NA	11.00
	Quantity	4	0	1	0	0	1

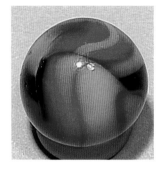

#182. Peltier Glass Company, Golden Rebel. 19/32". $500.

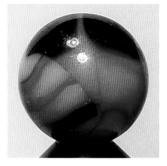

#183. Peltier Glass Company, Golden Rebel. 21/32". $750.

Peltier Glass Company
Golden Rebel

Up to:		9.9-9.7	9.6-9.3	9.2-9.0	8.9-8.5	8.4-8.0	7.9-7.0
5/8"	High	680.00	625.00	625.00	210.00	310.00	80.00
	Low	680.00	625.00	625.00	210.00	90.00	80.00
	Average	680.00	625.00	625.00	210.00	235.00	80.00
	Quantity	1	1	1	1	7	1
3/4"	High	NA	NA	780.00	NA	NA	NA
	Low	NA	NA	780.00	NA	NA	NA
	Average	NA	NA	780.00	NA	NA	NA
	Quantity	0	0	1	0	0	0
7/8"	High	3250.00	NA	1525.00	NA	NA	NA
	Low	3250.00	NA	1525.00	NA	NA	NA
	Average	3250.00	NA	1525.00	NA	NA	NA
	Quantity	1	0	1	0	0	0

#184. Peltier Glass Company, Ketchup and Mustard. 21/32". $75.

#185. Peltier Glass Company, Ketchup and Mustard. 3/4". $125.

Peltier Glass Company
Ketchup and Mustard

Up to:		9.9-9.7	9.6-9.3	9.2-9.0	8.9-8.5	8.4-8.0	7.9-7.0
5/8"	High	75.00	42.00	31.00	23.00	20.50	6.00
	Low	65.00	29.00	31.00	23.00	20.50	5.00
	Average	70.00	35.33	31.00	23.00	20.50	5.50
	Quantity	1	3	1	1	1	2
3/4"	High	NA	90.00	55.00	30.00	15.50	NA
	Low	NA	47.00	28.00	30.00	10.00	NA
	Average	NA	68.50	46.11	30.00	12.75	NA
	Quantity	0	2	9	1	2	0
7/8"	High	310.00	NA	NA	NA	NA	NA
	Low	310.00	NA	NA	NA	NA	NA
	Average	310.00	NA	NA	NA	NA	NA
	Quantity	1	0	0	0	0	0

#186. Peltier Glass Company, Liberty. 21/32". $25.

#187. Peltier Glass Company, Liberty. 5/8". $60.

Peltier Glass Company
Liberty

Up to:		9.9-9.7	9.6-9.3	9.2-9.0	8.9-8.5	8.4-8.0	7.9-7.0
5/8"	High	90.00	NA	55.00	37.00	NA	NA
	Low	37.00	NA	42.00	9.00	NA	NA
	Average	62.57	NA	48.50	23.00	NA	NA
	Quantity	7	0	2	2	0	0
3/4"	High	65.00	65.00	43.00	13.00	NA	NA
	Low	65.00	65.00	43.00	13.00	NA	NA
	Average	65.00	65.00	43.00	13.00	NA	NA
	Quantity	1	1	1	1	0	0
7/8"	High	385.00	NA	300.00	160.00	NA	NA
	Low	350.00	NA	300.00	160.00	NA	NA
	Average	368.00	NA	300.00	160.00	NA	NA
	Quantity	2	0	1	1	0	0

#188. Peltier Glass Company, Rebel. 21/32". $75.

#189. Peltier Glass Company, Rebel. 25/32". $200.

Peltier Glass Company
Rebel

Up to:		9.9-9.7	9.6-9.3	9.2-9.0	8.9-8.5	8.4-8.0	7.9-7.0
5/8"	High	95.00	110.00	50.00	22.00	7.50	7.00
	Low	95.00	50.00	42.00	15.00	7.50	7.00
	Average	95.00	68.75	45.33	19.50	7.50	7.00
	Quantity	1	4	3	3	1	1
3/4"	High	200.00	NA	130.00	NA	60.00	15.00
	Low	170.00	NA	130.00	NA	13.00	3.25
	Average	190.00	NA	130.00	NA	31.50	9.13
	Quantity	3	0	1	0	4	2
7/8"	High	NA	NA	NA	200.00	NA	NA
	Low	NA	NA	NA	47.00	NA	NA
	Average	NA	NA	NA	119.00	NA	NA
	Quantity	0	0	0	3	0	0

#190. Peltier Glass
Company, Superboy.
5/8". $75.

#191. Peltier Glass
Company, Superboy.
27/32". $1000.

Peltier Glass Company
Superboy

Up to:		9.9-9.7	9.6-9.3	9.2-9.0	8.9-8.5	8.4-8.0	7.9-7.0
5/8"	High	73.00	NA	45.00	21.00	NA	NA
	Low	37.00	NA	39.00	13.00	NA	NA
	Average	59.00	NA	42.00	17.00	NA	NA
	Quantity	3	0	2	2	0	0
3/4"	High	156.97	NA	NA	75.00	NA	25.00
	Low	111.00	NA	NA	75.00	NA	12.00
	Average	127.66	NA	NA	75.00	NA	18.50
	Quantity	3	0	0	1	0	2
7/8"	High	NA	NA	650.00	125.00	NA	NA
	Low	NA	NA	255.00	125.00	NA	NA
	Average	NA	NA	452.50	125.00	NA	NA
	Quantity	0	0	2	1	0	0

#192. Peltier Glass Company,
Superman. 5/8". $150.

#193. Peltier Glass Company,
Superman. 21/32". $175.

Peltier Glass Company
Superman

Up to:		9.9-9.7	9.6-9.3	9.2-9.0	8.9-8.5	8.4-8.0	7.9-7.0
5/8"	High	225.00	80.00	110.00	85.00	NA	NA
	Low	125.00	80.00	41.00	85.00	NA	NA
	Average	172.50	80.00	75.50	85.00	NA	NA
	Quantity	4	1	2	1	0	0
3/4"	High	450.00	490.00	185.00	180.00	NA	NA
	Low	450.00	80.00	185.00	30.00	NA	NA
	Average	450.00	285.00	185.00	105.00	NA	NA
	Quantity	1	2	1	2	0	0
7/8"	High	NA	NA	750.00	NA	NA	NA
	Low	NA	NA	310.00	NA	NA	NA
	Average	NA	NA	492.50	NA	NA	NA
	Quantity	0	0	4	0	0	0

#194. Peltier Glass
Company, Tiger. 5/8". $50.

#195. Peltier Glass
Company, Tiger. 5/8". $50.

Peltier Glass Company
Tiger

Up to:		9.9-9.7	9.6-9.3	9.2-9.0	8.9-8.5	8.4-8.0	7.9-7.0
5/8"	High	65.00	39.00	27.00	34.00	12.00	NA
	Low	47.00	39.00	15.00	8.00	5.00	NA
	Average	56.60	39.00	21.50	16.71	8.50	NA
	Quantity	5	1	6	7	2	0
3/4"	High	150.00	60.00	NA	50.00	NA	NA
	Low	40.00	29.00	NA	15.00	NA	NA
	Average	76.25	44.50	NA	26.67	NA	NA
	Quantity	4	2	0	3	0	0

#196. Peltier Glass
Company, Wasp.
21/32". $50.

#197. Peltier Glass
Company, Wasp. 5/8".
$50.

Peltier Glass Company
Wasp

Up to: 5/8"		9.9-9.7	9.6-9.3	9.2-9.0	8.9-8.5	8.4-8.0	7.9-7.0
	High	90.00	56.00	36.00	42.00	15.00	NA
	Low	50.00	39.00	20.00	17.00	5.00	NA
	Average	72.00	47.50	28.00	28.67	10.33	NA
	Quantity	5	2	2	3	3	0
3/4"	High	105.00	NA	NA	35.00	19.50	NA
	Low	105.00	NA	NA	35.00	19.50	NA
	Average	105.00	NA	NA	35.00	19.50	NA
	Quantity	1	0	0	1	1	0

#198. Peltier Glass
Company, Zebra. 3/4". $30.

#199. Peltier Glass
Company, Zebra. 11/16".
$25.

Peltier Glass Company
Zebra

Up to: 5/8"		9.9-9.7	9.6-9.3	9.2-9.0	8.9-8.5	8.4-8.0	7.9-7.0
	High	44.00	27.00	12.00	9.00	NA	NA
	Low	18.00	13.00	10.00	1.00	NA	NA
	Average	24.33	18.33	11.00	5.50	NA	NA
	Quantity	6	3	2	4	1	0

Size	Stat						
3/4"	High	95.00	65.00	61.00	26.00	NA	NA
	Low	23.00	13.00	9.00	1.00	NA	NA
	Average	28.50	21.67	17.60	12.00	NA	NA
	Quantity	5	6	5	3	0	0
7/8"	High	110.00	NA	NA	11.00	NA	NA
	Low	80.00	NA	NA	11.00	NA	NA
	Average	95.00	NA	NA	11.00	NA	NA
	Quantity	2	0	0	1	0	0

#200. Peltier Glass Company, National Line Rainbo. 21/32". $20.

#201. Peltier Glass Company, National Line Rainbo. 5/8". $25.

#202. Peltier Glass Company, National Line Rainbo. 3/4". $50.

#203. Peltier Glass Company, National Line Rainbo. 21/32". $75.

Other Peltier Glass Company Two-Color National Line Rainbo

Up to:		9.9-9.7	9.6-9.3	9.2-9.0	8.9-8.5	8.4-8.0	7.9-7.0
5/8"	High	65.00	31.00	23.00	37.00	13.00	NA
	Low	8.00	12.00	3.00	3.00	5.00	NA
	Average	22.14	17.50	12.68	10.83	9.44	NA
	Quantity	22	4	14	9	4	0
3/4"	High	120.00	21.00	80.00	26.00	17.45	11.00
	Low	10.00	21.00	4.00	3.25	1.00	0.50
	Average	41.00	21.00	15.71	12.33	9.91	4.00
	Quantity	9	1	21	12	6	3
7/8"	High	NA	65.00	65.00	60.00	NA	17.00
	Low	NA	65.00	17.00	2.00	NA	13.50
	Average	NA	65.00	39.43	31.85	NA	15.25
	Quantity	0	1	7	7	0	2

RAINBO

The more common ribboned Peltier marble is the Rainbo. This Rainbo is a more recent marble than the National Line Rainbo. As with the National Line Rainbo, these have a two seam design. The base glass can be a variety of opaque or transparent colors, depending on the particular type of Rainbo, and they all have a ribbon or pair of ribbons encircling the equator of the marble. There is a basic difference between a National Line Rainbo and a Rainbo. In a National Line Rainbo, the ribbons lay just on and below the surface of the marble. This is easily seen on a National Line Rainbo that has chips on the ribbons. In a Rainbo, the ribbons go into the marble, towards the core.

Examples with an opaque white base with a pair of colored ribbons encircling the equator are called Rainbos. Examples with a translucent white base with a pair of colored ribbons encircling the equator are called Acme Realers. An opalescent white base with a pair of red ribbons encircling the equator is called Bloodie. Marbles with bubble-filled transparent clear bases with a red and white, orange and white, or yellow and white pair of ribbons encircling the equator are called Sunsets. A transparent dark base with a yellow and white ribbon brushed on the equator of the marble is a Champion Jr. Marbles with an opaque colored base or transparent colored base with a pair of different colored ribbons encircling the equator are called Tri-colors. Transparent clear with ribbons of two or three different colors are called Clear Rainbos. There are also Rainbos with opaque white base and two different colors in the ribbons (similar to tri-color National Line Rainbos).

Many variations on the above basic marbles are turning up all the time, although Rainbos do not seem to have quite the variety of corkscrews. Some Rainbos have been found with six ribbons instead of four, and Rainbos with different colors on either side. The values for these variations were still volatile at the time this guide was revised.

In all, four different variations of design have been found in National Line Rainbos and Rainbos. The earliest are six ribbons that almost appear swirled (but still have two seams somewhere on the marble). These are tri-color National Line Rainbos. Four ribbon two-color National Line Rainbos, that have a swirling pattern to them (but, again, have two seams) are of the same vintage. These swirling type could be called "Type I National Line Rainbo." The more recent type of National Line Rainbo (still 1920s to 1930s) have six (tri-colors) or four (two-colors) ribbons that are fairly straight and have seams on either side of the marble. These could be referred to as "Type II National Line Rainbo." The earliest Rainbos have a ribbon on either hemisphere surrounding the equator and a patch on either pole. Six ribbon Rainbos are this variety too. These could be referred to as "Type I Rainbo." The more recent Rainbos have two ribbons on either hemisphere that surround the equator. These could be called "Type II Rainbo." Keep in mind that the ribbons on National Line Rainbos only lay on the surface or go just under the surface. The ribbons on Rainbos go much farther into the marble, sometimes all the way to the center.

#204. Peltier Glass Company, Bloodie. 5/8". $2.

#205. Peltier Glass Company, Bloodie. 5/8" & 25/32". $5 and 25.

Peltier Glass Company
Bloodie

Up to:		9.9-9.7	9.6-9.3	9.2-9.0	8.9-8.5	8.4-8.0	7.9-7.0
3/4"	High	10.50	NA	3.00	NA	NA	NA
	Low	3.00	NA	3.00	NA	NA	NA
	Average	5.83	NA	3.00	NA	NA	NA
	Quantity	3	0	1	0	0	0
1"	High	21.00	14.50	10.00	6.00	NA	NA
	Low	15.00	14.50	10.00	6.00	NA	NA
	Average	17.67	14.50	10.00	6.00	NA	NA
	Quantity	3	1	1	1	0	0

#206. Peltier Glass Company, Champion Jr. 5/8". $2.

Peltier Glass Company
Champion Jr.

Up to:		9.9-9.7	9.6-9.3	9.2-9.0	8.9-8.5	8.4-8.0	7.9-7.0
5/8"	High	2.00	NA	0.25	NA	NA	NA
	Low	0.50	NA	0.25	NA	NA	NA
	Average	1.25	NA	0.25	NA	NA	NA
	Quantity	2	0	1	0	0	0
3/4"	High	11.50	NA	NA	NA	NA	NA
	Low	1.00	NA	NA	NA	NA	NA
	Average	4.83	NA	NA	NA	NA	NA
	Quantity	3	0	0	0	0	0

#207. Peltier Glass
Company, Clear Rainbo.
19/32". $20.

#208. Peltier Glass
Company, Clear Rainbo.
19/32". $45.

Peltier Glass Company
Clear Rainbo

Up to:		9.9-9.7	9.6-9.3	9.2-9.0	8.9-8.5	8.4-8.0	7.9-7.0
5/8"	High	30.00	27.00	30.00	NA	NA	NA
	Low	30.00	27.00	18.00	NA	NA	NA
	Average	30.00	27.00	25.33	NA	NA	NA
	Quantity	1	1	3	0	0	0

#209. Peltier Glass Company,
Clown. 5/8". $35.

#210. Peltier Glass Company,
Clown. 7/8". $90.

Peltier Glass Company
Clown

Up to:		9.9-9.7	9.6-9.3	9.2-9.0	8.9-8.5	8.4-8.0	7.9-7.0
5/8"	High	35.00	27.00	15.00	NA	NA	NA
	Low	35.00	27.00	15.00	NA	NA	NA
	Average	35.00	27.00	15.00	NA	NA	NA
	Quantity	1	1	1	0	0	0

#211. Peltier Glass Company, Sunset. 5/8". $5.

#212. Peltier Glass Company, Sunset. 5/8". $5.

Peltier Glass Company
Sunset

Up to:		9.9-9.7	9.6-9.3	9.2-9.0	8.9-8.5	8.4-8.0	7.9-7.0
5/8"	High	6.00	NA	6.00	NA	NA	NA
	Low	6.00	NA	4.00	NA	NA	NA
	Average	6.00	NA	5.33	NA	NA	NA
	Quantity	1	0	3	0	0	0

#213. Peltier Glass Company, Rainbo. 5/8". $2.

#214. Peltier Glass Company, Rainbo. 25/32". $15.

Other Peltier Glass
Company Rainbos

Up to:		9.9-9.7	9.6-9.3	9.2-9.0	8.9-8.5	8.4-8.0	7.9-7.0
5/8"	High	4.00	1.25	9.00	1.00	NA	NA
	Low	1.00	1.25	0.25	0.50	NA	NA
	Average	2.34	1.25	0.80	0.75	NA	NA
	Quantity	20	1	6	4	0	0

3/4"	High	3.00	4.00	3.20	4.00	NA	NA
	Low	3.00	1.00	1.00	1.00	NA	NA
	Average	3.00	2.50	2.22	2.50	NA	NA
	Quantity	1	6	9	5	0	0
7/8"	High	15.50	7.00	10.00	5.50	NA	NA
	Low	5.00	7.00	1.00	2.00	NA	NA
	Average	10.25	7.00	4.20	3.60	NA	NA
	Quantity	2	1	4	3	0	0
1"	High	20.00	6.00	7.00	10.00	NA	NA
	Low	7.00	4.00	2.00	2.00	NA	NA
	Average	12.60	5.00	4.67	3.83	NA	NA
	Quantity	5	2	12	6	0	0

MULTICOLOR

Another type of Peltier ribbon marble is the Multicolor. These are transparent green (light to dark) with six ribbons, usually in three different colors.

#215. Peltier Glass Company, Multicolor. 21/32". $10.

#216. Peltier Glass Company, Multicolor. 21/32". $30.

#217. Peltier Glass Company, Multicolor. 11/16". $250.

Peltier Glass Company
Multicolor

Up to:		9.9-9.7	9.6-9.3	9.2-9.0	8.9-8.5	8.4-8.0	7.9-7.0
5/8"	High	13.00	6.25	7.00	2.00	NA	NA
	Low	1.00	2.00	2.00	1.00	NA	NA
	Average	6.32	4.75	4.17	1.80	NA	NA
	Quantity	23	3	6	5	0	0
3/4"	High	35.50	35.00	77.00	58.00	13.00	NA
	Low	4.00	4.00	1.00	2.00	13.00	NA
	Average	31.77	24.72	19.62	16.29	13.00	NA
	Quantity	24	6	12	6	1	0
7/8"	High	NA	NA	360.00	75.00	NA	NA
	Low	NA	NA	360.00	75.00	NA	NA
	Average	NA	NA	360.00	75.00	NA	NA
	Quantity	0	0	1	1	0	0

CAT'S-EYE

Peltier also produced a type of cat's-eye. The marble consists of a single-vaned opaque color in transparent clear glass. They are referred to as Bananas because the shape of the vane looks like a banana. These marbles are fairly common, although not as common as other American or foreign cat's-eyes. The most common colors for the vane are yellow, red, blue, green or white. These have minimal value and are not reported in the table below. Other colors are less common. The 9.9-9.7 marble reported below was in yellow glass. The 9.2-9.0 marble reported below was an aventurine green core.

#218. Peltier Glass Company, Banana. 19/32". $1.

#219. Peltier Glass Company, Banana. 19/32". $1.

Peltier Glass Company Cat's-eyes

Up to: 5/8"		9.9-9.7	9.6-9.3	9.2-9.0	8.9-8.5	8.4-8.0	7.9-7.0
	High	29.00	NA	12.00	NA	NA	NA
	Low	29.00	NA	12.00	NA	NA	NA
	Average	29.00	NA	12.00	NA	NA	NA
	Quantity	1	0	1	0	0	0

HONEY ONYX

There is a patch that is called a Honey Onyx. These have a semi-opaque white base with a thin translucent brown patch and a thin translucent green stripe on the marble. They are rare.

#220. Peltier Glass Company, Honey Onyx. 11/16". $75.

#221. Peltier Glass Company, Honey Onyx. 11/16". $75.

Peltier Glass Company
Honey Onyx

Up to:		9.9-9.7	9.6-9.3	9.2-9.0	8.9-8.5	8.4-8.0	7.9-7.0
5/8"	High	80.00	NA	NA	NA	NA	NA
	Low	80.00	NA	NA	NA	NA	NA
	Average	80.00	NA	NA	NA	NA	NA
	Quantity	1	0	0	0	0	0
3/4"	High	180.00	NA	NA	NA	NA	NA
	Low	90.00	NA	NA	NA	NA	NA
	Average	135.00	NA	NA	NA	NA	NA
	Quantity	2	0	0	0	0	0

ROOT BEER FLOAT

There is also a type of Peltier cat's-eye that is similar to the Banana. These were only produced for a short period of time. They have a transparent dark amber base with a flat wide white vane in the middle. They are sometimes referred to by marble collectors as a Peltier Root Beer Float and have only been found in the 11/16" to 7/8" size. They were a limited run.

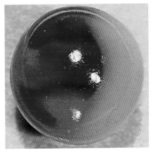

#222. Peltier Glass Company, Root Beer Float. 7/8". $50.

#223. Peltier Glass Company, Root Beer Float. 7/8". $50.

Peltier Glass Company
Root Beer Float

Up to:		9.9-9.7	9.6-9.3	9.2-9.0	8.9-8.5	8.4-8.0	7.9-7.0
1"	High	110.00	19.00	NA	NA	NA	NA
	Low	55.00	19.00	NA	NA	NA	NA
	Average	82.50	19.00	NA	NA	NA	NA
	Quantity	15	1	0	0	0	0

NOVA

Another limited run marble is the Peltier Nova. These have a white or black base with two patches of color.

#224. Peltier Glass Company, Nova. 7/8". $25.

#225. Peltier Glass Company, Nova. 7/8". $10.

Peltier Glass Company
Nova

Up to: 1"		9.9-9.7	9.6-9.3	9.2-9.0	8.9-8.5	8.4-8.0	7.9-7.0
	High	35.00	25.00	NA	NA	NA	NA
	Low	11.00	5.00	NA	NA	NA	NA
	Average	21.25	12.33	NA	NA	NA	NA
	Quantity	4	3	0	0	0	0

THE MASTER MARBLE COMPANY/ THE MASTER GLASS COMPANY

The Master Marble Company was founded in 1930 by four former employees of the Akro Agate Company. The company closed in 1941 and the machinery was purchased by one of the former owners, who formed The Master Glass Company. Master Glass closed in 1973.

The Master Marble Company used machinery which was similar to Akro Agate's, but most notably, did not include the Freese improvement which offset the rollers. This means that Master marbles have a crimp or feathering mark at either pole. Also, due to the design of the machinery, Master marbles have a unique pattern at either end. At either end you can see a small "V" of the color on one side of the marble indenting into the color on the other side.

115

SUNBURST

The most collectible Master marble is the Sunburst (also very collectible is a related marble called the Tiger-Eye). The Sunburst was an attempt to duplicate handmade onionskins. The marble has a transparent clear base with filaments and strands of various colors running from pole to pole and completely filling the marble. Some Sunbursts have clear patches or areas in them. A Tiger-Eye is a Sunburst that is almost completely clear. It has filaments and strands forming a wide, flat ribbon in the center of the marble. They are rarer than Sunbursts. The colors are usually orange, white, and black in a transparent clear base.

 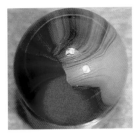 

#226. Master Marble Company, Sunburst. 11/16". $20.

#227. Master Marble Company, Sunburst. 21/32". $15.

#228. Master Marble Company, Sunburst. 11/16". $5.

 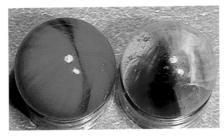

#229. Master Marble Company, Sunburst. 21/32". $5.

Master Glass Company, Sunburst.

Master Marble Company Sunbursts

Up to: 5/8"		9.9-9.7	9.6-9.3	9.2-9.0	8.9-8.5	8.4-8.0	7.9-7.0
	High	23.00	9.00	11.00	1.00	NA	NA
	Low	2.00	9.00	6.00	1.00	NA	NA
	Average	9.46	9.00	8.40	1.00	NA	NA
	Quantity	15	1	5	1	0	0
3/4"	High	27.50	16.00	19.00	8.00	200	NA
	Low	11.00	12.00	8.00	1.00	2.00	NA
	Average	17.73	14.33	12.33	3.00	2.00	NA
	Quantity	21	3	6	4	1	0

#230. Master Marble
Company, Tiger-Eye.
11/16". $20.

#231. Master Marble
Company, Tiger-Eye.
21/32". $15.

Master Marble Company
Tiger-Eye

Up to:		9.9-9.7	9.6-9.3	9.2-9.0	8.9-8.5	8.4-8.0	7.9-7.0
5/8"	High	25.00	NA	12.50	NA	NA	NA
	Low	11.00	NA	8.00	NA	NA	NA
	Average	20.60	NA	10.20	NA	NA	NA
	Quantity	5	0	3	0	0	0
3/4"	High	25.00	NA	NA	7.00	NA	NA
	Low	25.00	NA	NA	4.00	NA	NA
	Average	25.00	NA	NA	5.50	NA	NA
	Quantity	1	0	0	2	0	0

PATCHES

Master Marble also made some patch marbles that are collectible. These patches were marketed under a variety of names, including Meteor (wispy translucent patch on opaque base), Comet (opaque patch on opaque base), and Cloudy (translucent patch on translucent base). The Master Marble patches are identifiable by a "V" or "U" pattern and feathering seen at each pole. The patches were made in a variety of patterns, including two-color opaque, two-color translucent, and opaque with a second color brushed on. Master Marbles' colors are fairly unique, although generally duller than Akro's.

#232. Master Marble
Company, Comet. 5/8" &
11/16". $2.50 and 5.

#233. Master Marble
Company, Comet. 5/8" &
21/32". $2 each.

#234. Master Marble
Company, Meteor. 5/8". $5.

#235. Master Marble
Company, Meteor.
5/8". $5.

#236. Master Marble
Company, Opaque.
11/16". $15.

#237. Master
Marble Company,
Cloudie. 21/32". $5.

Master Marble Company Patches

Up to:		9.9-9.7	9.6-9.3	9.2-9.0	8.9-8.5	8.4-8.0	7.9-7.0
5/8"	High	7.00	NA	5.00	3.00	NA	NA
	Low	1.00	NA	2.00	0.25	NA	NA
	Average	3.92	NA	3.50	1.41	NA	NA
	Quantity	11	0	2	3	0	0
3/4"	High	30.00	NA	4.00	2.90	NA	NA
	Low	2.00	NA	4.00	0.50	NA	NA
	Average	8.04	NA	4.00	1.53	NA	NA
	Quantity	26	0	2	6	0	0

OPAQUE AND CLEARIE

Master Marble and Master Glass made a variety of clearies, opaques, and cat's-eyes (Master Glass only). Master clearies and opaques all have the typical "V" or "U" pattern at either end. Many are the same colors as those made by other companies. However, there are several colors that are unique to Master. These include a semi-opaque to translucent purple and a semi-opaque to translucent green, and are reported below.

Master Marble Company and Master Glass Company Opaques and Clearies

Up to: 3/4"		9.9-9.7	9.6-9.3	9.2-9.0	8.9-8.5	8.4-8.0	7.9-7.0
	High	22.00	9.00	NA	NA	NA	NA
	Low	4.00	9.00	NA	NA	NA	NA
	Average	11.33	9.00	NA	NA	NA	NA
	Quantity	3	1	0	0	0	0

CAT'S-EYE

Master cat's-eyes are typically single color translucent three vane varieties in transparent clear glass. There is also a harder to find single vane variety. The marbles reported below have aventurine green cores, or oxblood in the core.

#239. Master Glass Company, Cat's-eye. 5/8". $1.

#240. Master Glass Company, Cat's-eye. 5/8". $50.

Master Glass Company Cat's-eye

Up to: 5/8"		9.9-9.7	9.6-9.3	9.2-9.0	8.9-8.5	8.4-8.0	7.9-7.0
	High	37.00	NA	13.00	8.00	NA	NA
	Low	12.00	NA	13.00	8.00	NA	NA
	Average	22.80	NA	13.00	8.00	NA	NA
	Quantity	5	0	1	1	0	0

ALLEY AGATE COMPANY

Lawrence Alley operated factories in at least four different locations in West Virginia (Paden City, Sisterville, Pennsboro, and St. Mary's) between 1929 and 1949. He also may have operated a plant in Salem, West Virginia. In 1949, he sold the St. Mary's plant to Berry Pink and Sellers Peltier, and they changed the company name to Marble King.

Alley produced a large variety of two and three color swirls, as well as one color opaques and clearies. They also produced a very small size marble, 3/8" in diameter. More research is needed in order to positively identify the unique marbles that Alley made. It is known that Alley produced marbles using a metallic color, as well as an oxblood. He also produced sets of children's dishes, similar to those made by Akro, including the Orphan Annie sets.

#241. Alley Agate Company, Swirl. 21/32". $50.

#243. Alley Agate Company, Swirl. 9/16". $10.

#242. Alley Agate Company, Swirl. 5/8". $5.

#244. Alley Agate Company, Swirl. 3/8". $200 all.

Alley Agate Company
Swirls

Up to: 5/8"		9.9-9.7	9.6-9.3	9.2-9.0	8.9-8.5	8.4-8.0	7.9-7.0
	High	22.00	7.00	5.00	2.00	NA	NA
	Low	4.00	7.00	1.00	2.00	NA	NA
	Average	11.20	7.00	2.28	2.00	NA	NA
	Quantity	17	1	7	1	0	0
3/4"	High	16.00	NA	NA	4.00	2.00	NA
	Low	16.00	NA	NA	2.25	2.00	NA
	Average	16.00	NA	NA	3.08	2.00	NA
	Quantity	1	0	0	3	1	0

MARBLE KING, INC.

Marble King was started in 1949 by Berry Pink and Sellers Peltier in St. Mary's, West Virginia. It was moved to Paden City, West Virginia, in 1958 after a fire destroyed the original plant. The machinery was purchased from the Alley Glass Company. Berry Pink had also been jobbing marbles since the 1920s under the trade name "Berry Pink, Inc."

Marble King produced ribboned, patch & ribboned, cat's-eye, and swirl marbles. Most are collectible today.

RAINBOW

Patch & ribbon marbles have a patch on one pole, a ribbon of a second color encircling the marble, a ribbon of the same color as the top patch encircling the marble, and finally a patch of the second color on the bottom pole. The marbles have two seams. They are made using a veneering method, which puts a thin layer of the colored glass on a base of white glass. These marbles were marketed under the name "Rainbows."

The most common Rainbow is white alternating with another color. The second color is usually red, blue, brown or green. There are Rainbows that are white with a color ribbon and patch consisting of two or three different colors. These are rarer. The most collectible Rainbows are two different alternating colors (not white). These have descriptive names that have been given to them by collectors. In ascending order of rarity are: Bumblebee (yellow & black), Wasp (red & black), Cub Scout (blue & yellow), Girl Scout (green & yellow), Tiger (orange & yellow), Spiderman (red & blue), Green Hornet (green & black), Watermelon (red & green), Dragonfly (green and blue). There are also hybrid examples that are either a patch or consist of three or four colors. These are very rare. Spidermen, Green Hornets, Watermelons, and Dragonflies have only been found in the 5/8" size. Girl Scouts and Tigers have only been found up to 3/4". Larger examples (up to 1") exist of the other types.

121

Some experimental Marble King Rainbows have surfaced that have a completely transparent clear base with one color patch and Ribboned on the surface. These are very rare and difficult to value

Another collectible Marble King marble is the Rainbow Red. This is a white base marble with an equatorial ribbon of red and a second equatorial ribbon of a different color, rather than a patch.

There are several types of new marbles being produced, or that have been recently produced, that are very similar to vintage Rainbows in terms of color and pattern. These include Rainbow-looking marbles that have a translucent base, Rainbow-looking marbles that are missing the patch but have the equatorial ribbon, and Rainbow-looking marbles where the two colors are blended together in thin strands or bands. None of these have much value.

#245. Marble King, Inc.,
Bumblebee. 5/8". $1.

Marble King Bumblebee

Up to:		9.9-9.7	9.6-9.3	9.2-9.0	8.9-8.5	8.4-8.0	7.9-7.0
5/8"	High	3.00	2.25	NA	NA	NA	NA
	Low	0.25	0.25	NA	NA	NA	NA
	Average	0.96	0.81	NA	NA	NA	NA
	Quantity	31	17	0	0	0	0
3/4"	High	8.00	NA	1.00	NA	NA	NA
	Low	2.00	NA	0.50	NA	NA	NA
	Average	3.55	NA	0.81	NA	NA	NA
	Quantity	15	0	12	0	0	0
1"	High	25.00	25.00	5.00	4.00	NA	NA
	Low	3.00	5.00	5.00	1.00	NA	NA
	Average	7.41	6.73	5.00	2.50	NA	NA
	Quantity	16	19	1	2	0	0

#246. Marble King,
Inc., Cub Scout. 5/8".
$2.

Marble King Cub Scout

Up to:		9.9-9.7	9.6-9.3	9.2-9.0	8.9-8.5	8.4-8.0	7.9-7.0
5/8"	High	3.00	NA	NA	0.25	NA	NA
	Low	1.00	NA	NA	0.25	NA	NA
	Average	2.25	NA	NA	0.25	NA	NA
	Quantity	25	0	0	1	0	0
3/4"	High	7.00	7.00	NA	4.00	NA	NA
	Low	5.00	4.00	NA	3.00	NA	NA
	Average	5.83	5.50	NA	3.50	NA	NA
	Quantity	3	2	0	2	0	0
1"	High	12.00	7.00	9.00	5.00	NA	NA
	Low	6.00	7.00	4.00	5.00	NA	NA
	Average	10.00	7.00	6.60	5.00	NA	NA
	Quantity	3	1	10	1	0	0

#247. Marble King, Inc.,
Girl Scout. 5/8". $10.

Marble King Girl Scout

Up to:		9.9-9.7	9.6-9.3	9.2-9.0	8.9-8.5	8.4-8.0	7.9-7.0
5/8"	High	13.00	13.00	7.00	5.00	NA	NA
	Low	5.00	7.00	5.00	5.00	NA	NA
	Average	10.22	9.50	6.00	5.00	NA	NA
	Quantity	19	10	2	1	0	0

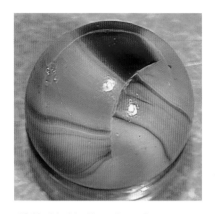

#248. Marble King, Inc., Green
Hornet. 5/8". $750.

Marble King Green Hornet

Up to: 5/8"		9.9-9.7	9.6-9.3	9.2-9.0	8.9-8.5	8.4-8.0	7.9-7.0
	High	600.00	NA	NA	NA	NA	NA
	Low	450.00	NA	NA	NA	NA	NA
	Average	525.00	NA	NA	NA	NA	NA
	Quantity	2	0	0	0	0	0

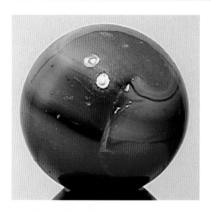

#249. Marble King, Inc., Spiderman.
19/32". $200.

Marble King Spiderman

Up to: 5/8"		9.9-9.7	9.6-9.3	9.2-9.0	8.9-8.5	8.4-8.0	7.9-7.0
	High	460.00	200.00	NA	NA	NA	NA
	Low	185.00	200.00	NA	NA	NA	NA
	Average	251.25	200.00	NA	NA	NA	NA
	Quantity	4	1	0	0	0	0

#250. Marble King,
Inc., Tiger. 5/8". $15.

Marble King Tiger

Up to:		9.9-9.7	9.6-9.3	9.2-9.0	8.9-8.5	8.4-8.0	7.9-7.0
5/8"	High	15.00	7.00	NA	NA	NA	NA
	Low	7.00	7.00	NA	NA	NA	NA
	Average	10.00	7.00	NA	NA	NA	NA
	Quantity	7	1	0	0	0	0
3/4"	High	31.00	NA	NA	NA	NA	NA
	Low	31.00	NA	NA	NA	NA	NA
	Average	31.00	NA	NA	NA	NA	NA
	Quantity	1	0	0	0	0	0

#251. Marble King, Inc.,
Wasp. 5/8". $2.

Marble King Wasp

Up to:		9.9-9.7	9.6-9.3	9.2-9.0	8.9-8.5	8.4-8.0	7.9-7.0
5/8"	High	4.00	2.00	NA	NA	NA	NA
	Low	1.00	1.00	NA	NA	NA	NA
	Average	2.66	1.75	NA	NA	NA	NA
	Quantity	6	4	0	0	0	0
3/4"	High	11.00	NA	NA	NA	NA	NA
	Low	7.00	NA	NA	NA	NA	NA
	Average	9.00	NA	NA	NA	NA	NA
	Quantity	2	0	0	0	0	0

7/8"	High	24.00	NA	10.00	NA	NA	NA
	Low	10.00	NA	10.00	NA	NA	NA
	Average	12.50	NA	10.00	NA	NA	NA
	Quantity	5	0	1	0	0	0

#252. Marble King, Inc.,
Watermelon. 5/8". $400.

Marble King Watermelon

Up to:		9.9-9.7	9.6-9.3	9.2-9.0	8.9-8.5	8.4-8.0	7.9-7.0
5/8"	High	650.00	NA	NA	NA	NA	NA
	Low	400.00	NA	NA	NA	NA	NA
	Average	525.00	NA	NA	NA	NA	NA
	Quantity	2	0	0	0	0	0

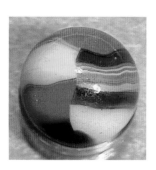

#253. Marble King, Inc.,
Rainbow Red. 5/8". $2.

#254. Marble King, Inc., Rainbow Red.
5/8". $2 each.

Marble King Rainbow Red

Up to:		9.9-9.7	9.6-9.3	9.2-9.0	8.9-8.5	8.4-8.0	7.9-7.0
5/8"	High	3.00	2.50	NA	NA	NA	NA
	Low	0.25	0.25	NA	NA	NA	NA
	Average	2.17	1.56	NA	NA	NA	NA
	Quantity	6	8	0	0	0	0
3/4"	High	6.00	NA	2.00	NA	NA	NA
	Low	0.50	NA	0.25	NA	NA	NA
	Average	4.55	NA	0.65	NA	NA	NA
	Quantity	5	0	4	0	0	0

255. Marble King, Inc., Rainbow. 15/16". $5.

256. Marble King, Inc., Rainbow. 5/8". $0.1.

257. Marble King, Inc., Rainbow. 5/8". $10.

258. Marble King, Inc., Rainbow (newer). 1/2". $10 each.

Marble King White-Base Rainbow

Up to:		9.9-9.7	9.6-9.3	9.2-9.0	8.9-8.5	8.4-8.0	7.9-7.0
5/8"	High	14.00	5.00	NA	2.00	NA	NA
	Low	2.00	1.00	NA	2.00	NA	NA
	Average	6.81	3.60	NA	2.00	NA	NA
	Quantity	8	4	0	1	0	0
3/4"	High	23.00	NA	3.00	NA	NA	NA
	Low	3.00	NA	2.00	NA	NA	NA
	Average	9.17	NA	2.50	NA	NA	NA
	Quantity	12	0	2	0	0	0

BLENDED

A Marble King Blended is similar to a Rainbow. It is a two-seam marble that appears to be a patch and ribbon. In fact, the surface veneer is two colors that are mixed together and completely cover the white base. The most common of these are Cub Scout (blue and yellow), Girl Scout (green and yellow), and Spiderman (blue and red).

259. Marble King, Inc., Blended. 19/32". $10.

260. Marble King, Inc., Blended. 19/32". $10 to 20 each.

Marble King Blended

Up to:		9.9-9.7	9.6-9.3	9.2-9.0	8.9-8.5	8.4-8.0	7.9-7.0
5/8"	High	60.00	NA	NA	NA	NA	NA
	Low	5.00	NA	NA	NA	NA	NA
	Average	24.97	NA	NA	NA	NA	NA
	Quantity	8	0	0	0	0	0

BERRY PINK PATCH

There is a marble that has been referred to as the Berry Pink Patch. It is uncertain whether this marble was actually produced by Marble King, but they are rare. The marble is transparent clear partially filled with white, with a patch of light blue and pink on one side. It has two seams.

261. Marble King, Inc., Berry Pink. 7/8". $75.

Marble King Berry Pink

Up to:		9.9-9.7	9.6-9.3	9.2-9.0	8.9-8.5	8.4-8.0	7.9-7.0
1"	High	NA	NA	70.00	112.00	NA	NA
	Low	NA	NA	65.00	40.00	NA	NA
	Average	NA	NA	66.66	64.20	NA	NA
	Quantity	0	0	3	10	0	0

CAT'S-EYE

Marble King has produced two types of cat's-eyes. The oldest (about 1950-1955) are called St. Mary's Cat's-eyes, because they were produced at the St. Mary's plant. These are four vane where two opposing vanes are one color and the other two opposing vanes are a different color. Most common are blue and yellow, but other combinations are known.

The other type of cat's-eye produced by Marble King is a four vane cat's-eye in a single color. These have minimal value. The other cat's-eyes reported in the table below have aventurine green vanes.

262. Marble King, Inc., St. Mary's Cat's-eye. 5/8". $10.

263. Marble King, Inc., St. Mary's Cat's-eye. 5/8". $30.

Marble King St. Mary's Cat's-eye

Up to:		9.9-9.7	9.6-9.3	9.2-9.0	8.9-8.5	8.4-8.0	7.9-7.0
5/8"	High	65.00	25.00	NA	NA	NA	NA
	Low	8.00	4.00	NA	NA	NA	NA
	Average	15.51	11.65	NA	NA	NA	NA
	Quantity	13	5	0	0	0	0

Up to:		9.9-9.7	9.6-9.3	9.2-9.0	8.9-8.5	8.4-8.0	7.9-7.0
5/8"	High	17.00	NA	NA	NA	NA	NA
	Low	0.25	NA	NA	NA	NA	NA
	Average	8.36	NA	NA	NA	NA	NA
	Quantity	47	0	0	0	0	0

264. Marble King, Inc., Cat's-eye. 5/8". $1.

265. Marble King, Inc., Cat's-eye. 5/8". $1.

RAVENSWOOD
NOVELTY WORKS

The Ravenswood Novelty Company began operations during 1931 or 1932, under the guidance of John Turnbull. Operations ended around 1954 or 1955, although the company is reported to have been making industrial marbles through 1959. During the late 1950s, Ravenswood was a major supplier of marbles to Krylon Paint for their aerosol cans. It is believed that they purchased these marbles from Vitro Agate Company.

The company made transparent and opaque swirls There is also strong evidence to suggest that they made the 1" Buddy marbles and did not buy them from Master Glass, as had been previously believed.

Ravenswood swirls are very unique in terms of coloring and design. Many of the Ravenswood designs and coloring are very similar. Ravenswood only produced marbles in the 9/16" to 5/8" size.

266. Ravenswood Novelty Company, Swirl. 19/32". $10.

267. Ravenswood Novelty Company, Swirl. 19/32". $2 each.

268. Ravenswood Novelty Company, Swirl. 5/8". $20.

269. Ravenswood Novelty Company, Swirl. 15/16". $10.

Ravenswood Novelty Works Swirls

Up to:		9.9-9.7	9.6-9.3	9.2-9.0	8.9-8.5	8.4-8.0	7.9-7.0
5/8"	High	25.00	12.00	6.00	NA	NA	NA
	Low	2.00	2.00	1.00	NA	NA	NA
	Average	18.25	8.13	3.50	NA	NA	NA
	Quantity	12	4	2	0	0	0
3/4"	High	17.00	NA	NA	NA	NA	NA
	Low	12.00	NA	NA	NA	NA	NA
	Average	14.50	NA	NA	NA	NA	NA
	Quantity	2	0	0	0	0	0
7/8"	High	26.00	NA	31.00	NA	NA	NA
	Low	26.00	NA	10.00	NA	NA	NA
	Average	26.00	NA	20.50	NA	NA	NA
	Quantity	1	NA	2	0	0	0
1"	High	23.00	NA	8.00	7.00	1.00	NA
	Low	8.00	NA	6.00	1.00	1.00	NA
	Average	13.00	NA	6.70	3.00	1.00	NA
	Quantity	8	NA	3	5	1	0

VITRO AGATE COMPANY/ GLADDING-VITRO AGATE COMPANY

The Vitro Agate Company began operations in 1932 in Parkersburg, West Virginia. It was acquired in 1969 by The Gladding Corporation, which changed the name to Gladding-Vitro Agate Company. In 1982, Gladding-Vitro was purchased by Paris Manufacturing Company, which changed the name back to Vitro Agate. In 1987, it was purchased by Viking Rope Company, which retained the name but moved the company to Anacortes, Washington. The company ceased operations in 1993 and the machinery and name were purchased by JABO, Inc. sometime after that. It then became JABO-Vitro Agate Company.

Early Vitro Agate marbles are the brushed variety. This is the type that has a thin layer of colored glass brushed on a base color. There are also a few veneered varieties, but these were manufactured later on.

More recently, Vitro Agate also made some two-seam marbles that are similar to Marble King Rainbows. They are readily identifiable because the marbles always have a defined crimp design at the seam between the two halves. Marble King's marbles do not have this crimp. Vitro also produced a number of two seam multicolor patch marbles. Many of these have clear and wispy white as one of the colors. When viewed ninety degrees from the seam, many have a stylized "V" pattern to them.

CONQUEROR

The Conqueror has a transparent clear base with a brushed surface patch. The remainder of the marble is brushed with opaque white. There is another type of marble that is similar to a Conqueror. It looks just like a Conqueror, but most of the interior of the marble is filled with translucent white filaments (occasionally the marble is opalescent). These are often referred to as "phantom conquerors." They are much more common than the Conqueror and have minimal value.

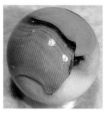

271. Vitro Agate Company, Conqueror. 3/4". $10.

272. Vitro Agate Company, Conqueror. 3/4". $10.

270. Vitro Agate Company, Conqueror. 5/8". $1 each.

273. Vitro Agate Company, Conqueror. 25/32". $10.

Vitro Agate Company
Conqueror

Up to:		9.9-9.7	9.6-9.3	9.2-9.0	8.9-8.5	8.4-8.0	7.9-7.0
5/8"	High	10.00	2.50	3.00	NA	NA	NA
	Low	0.25	1.00	1.00	NA	NA	NA
	Average	4.35	1.75	2.25	NA	NA	NA
	Quantity	13	2	5	0	0	0
3/4"	High	12.00	NA	6.00	4.00	NA	NA
	Low	3.00	NA	6.00	4.00	NA	NA
	Average	5.90	NA	6.00	4.00	NA	NA
	Quantity	9	0	1	1	0	0

HELMET PATCH

A Helmet Patch looks just like a football helmet on a head. The patch is an opaque color, usually white, with a colored stripe down the middle, and looks just like a football helmet. The head is a transparent or translucent color, often green or brown.

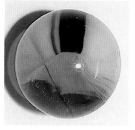

274. Vitro Agate Company, Helmet Patch. 5/8". $2.5.

275. Vitro Agate Company, Helmet Patch. 3/4". $15.

Vitro Agate Company
Helmet Patch

Up to:		9.9-9.7	9.6-9.3	9.2-9.0	8.9-8.5	8.4-8.0	7.9-7.0
5/8"	High	5.50	NA	NA	NA	NA	NA
	Low	0.25	NA	NA	NA	NA	NA
	Average	1.66	NA	NA	NA	NA	NA
	Quantity	25	0	0	0	0	0
3/4"	High	12.00	NA	NA	NA	NA	NA
	Low	12.00	NA	NA	NA	NA	NA
	Average	12.00	NA	NA	NA	NA	NA
	Quantity	1	0	0	0	0	0

PARROT

A Parrot is an opaque white base with three or four colored patches on the surface. The more desirable example has four patches completely covering the marble, one of which is aventurine green. There are examples that leave a lot of white showing. These are less desirable.

276. Vitro Agate Company, Parrot. 21/32". $20.

277. Vitro Agate Company, Parrot. 7/8". $75.

278. Vitro Agate Company, Oxblood Patch. 5/8". $20.

279. Vitro Agate Company, Parrot. 7/8". $75.

Vitro Agate Company
Parrot

Up to:		9.9-9.7	9.6-9.3	9.2-9.0	8.9-8.5	8.4-8.0	7.9-7.0
3/4"	High	110.00	NA	80.00	32.00	NA	NA
	Low	34.00	NA	50.00	32.00	NA	NA
	Average	65.55	NA	65.00	32.00	NA	NA
	Quantity	9	0	2	1	0	0
15/16"	High	185.00	NA	120.00	NA	NA	NA
	Low	44.00	NA	30.00	NA	NA	NA
	Average	82.12	NA	67.11	NA	NA	NA
	Quantity	17	0	9	0	0	0

POPEYE PATCH

A Popeye Patch is transparent clear with filaments of white filling it. There is a patch on the surface of two colors, almost always blue and yellow. It looks just like a Popeye corkscrew that has not spun. However, it was made by Vitro, not by Akro.

280. Vitro Agate Company, Popeye Patch. 19/32". $1.

Vitro Agate Company
Popeye Patch

Up to:		9.9-9.7	9.6-9.3	9.2-9.0	8.9-8.5	8.4-8.0	7.9-7.0
5/8"	High	4.50	NA	NA	NA	NA	NA
	Low	0.25	NA	NA	NA	NA	NA
	Average	2.69	NA	NA	NA	NA	NA
	Quantity	4	0	0	0	0	0

ALL-RED

The most common Vitro Agate patch is the All-Red. There are two varieties of this marble. Both are opaque white base. Each has patches at the poles, usually two different colors. The older type has a black ribbon between the two patches. The more recent type does not.

281. Vitro Agate Company, All-Red. 25/32". $5 to 15 each.

282. Vitro Agate Company, All-Red. 5/8". $0.1.

283. Vitro Agate Company, All-Red. 5/8". $2 each.

284. Vitro Agate Company, All-Red. 25/32". $15.

Vitro Agate Company
All-Red

Up to: 7/8"		9.9-9.7	9.6-9.3	9.2-9.0	8.9-8.5	8.4-8.0	7.9-7.0
	High	22.00	NA	17.00	2.00	NA	NA
	Low	0.25	NA	3.00	2.00	NA	NA
	Average	9.89	NA	7.67	2.00	NA	NA
	Quantity	9	0	3	1	0	0
1"	High	18.00	NA	23.00	3.00	NA	NA
	Low	3.25	NA	1.00	3.00	NA	NA
	Average	12.42	NA	11.66	3.00	NA	NA
	Quantity	13	0	6	1	0	0

285. Vitro Agate Company, Patch. 7/8". $25.

286. Vitro Agate Company, Patch. 7/8". $5.

Other Vitro Agate Patches

Up to:		9.9-9.7	9.6-9.3	9.2-9.0	8.9-8.5	8.4-8.0	7.9-7.0
5/8"	High	7.00	2.00	2.00	1.00	NA	NA
	Low	0.25	0.25	0.75	1.00	NA	NA
	Average	2.18	1.13	0.94	1.00	NA	NA
	Quantity	14	2	5	3	0	0
3/4"	High	11.00	8.00	8.00	NA	NA	NA
	Low	2.00	1.00	1.00	NA	NA	NA
	Average	6.20	2.21	1.25	NA	NA	NA
	Quantity	5	5	4	0	0	0
1"	Low	24.00	5.00	NA	3.00	NA	NA
	High	2.00	5.00	NA	2.00	NA	NA
	Average	11.67	5.00	NA	2.50	NA	NA
	Quantity	6	1	0	2	0	0

WHITIE

A Whitie is a two-seam opaque white marble with a colored ribbon around the equator. In some cases, the ribbon is aventurine green.

287. Vitro Agate Company, Whitie. 5/8". $1.

Vitro Agate Company
Whitie

Up to: 5/8"		9.9-9.7	9.6-9.3	9.2-9.0	8.9-8.5	8.4-8.0	7.9-7.0
	High	3.00	NA	NA	2.00	NA	NA
	Low	2.00	NA	NA	2.00	NA	NA
	Average	2.50	NA	NA	2.00	NA	NA
	Quantity	2	0	0	1	0	0

288. Vitro Agate Company,
Whitie (aventurine). 5/8". $5.

BLACKIE

A Blackie is a two-seam opaque black marble with a colored ribbon brushed around the equator.

Vitro Agate Company
Blackie

Up to: 5/8"		9.9-9.7	9.6-9.3	9.2-9.0	8.9-8.5	8.4-8.0	7.9-7.0
	High	12.00	NA	NA	2.00	NA	NA
	Low	2.00	NA	NA	2.00	NA	NA
	Average	7.40	NA	NA	2.00	NA	NA
	Quantity	12	0	0	1	0	0

8-FINGER RIBBON

A Vitro 8-Finger Ribbon is a two-seam marble. It has a transparent (green, red, yellow, clear) or opaque (black) base with eight opaque white ribbons in the marble.

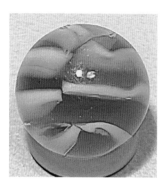

289. Vitro Agate Company, Ribbon - 8 Finger. 19/32". $45.

Vitro Agate Company
8-Finger Ribbon

Up to:		9.9-9.7	9.6-9.3	9.2-9.0	8.9-8.5	8.4-8.0	7.9-7.0
5/8"	High	85.00	NA	NA	NA	NA	NA
	Low	12.00	NA	NA	NA	NA	NA
	Average	31.00	NA	NA	NA	NA	NA
	Quantity	20	0	0	0	0	0

290. Vitro Agate Company, Ribbon - Other. 19/32". $1.

Other Vitro Agate Company Ribboned

Up to:		9.9-9.7	9.6-9.3	9.2-9.0	8.9-8.5	8.4-8.0	7.9-7.0
5/8"	High	13.00	1.00	1.00	NA	NA	NA
	Low	3.75	1.00	1.00	NA	NA	NA
	Average	8.40	1.00	1.00	NA	NA	NA
	Quantity	4	1	1	0	0	0

CAT'S-EYE

Vitro Agate has made several kinds of cat's-eyes. One type is four or five vane in clear. Some of these have aventurine vanes. Others have vanes that are one color, edged by a second color (hybrids). Usually the vanes are all one color and these have minimal value. A cat's-eye, produced by Gladding-Vitro Agate, is the cage style. This is a transparent clear or transparent aqua base with six to eight subsurface narrow colored bands.

291. Vitro Agate Company, Cat's-eye (hybrid). 5/8". $2.

292. Vitro Agate Company, Cat's-eye. 5/8". $1.

293. Vitro Agate Company, Cat's-eye. 7/8". $40.

Vitro Agate Company Cat's-eye

Up to:		9.9-9.7	9.6-9.3	9.2-9.0	8.9-8.5	8.4-8.0	7.9-7.0
5/8"	High	12.00	NA	NA	NA	NA	NA
	Low	0.25	NA	NA	NA	NA	NA
	Average	1.43	NA	NA	NA	NA	NA
	Quantity	36	0	0	0	0	0
7/8"	High	35.00	NA	NA	NA	NA	NA
	Low	1.00	NA	NA	NA	NA	NA
	Average	8.50	NA	NA	NA	NA	NA
	Quantity	15	0	0	0	0	0

CHAMPION AGATE COMPANY

The Champion Agate Company began operations in Pennsboro, West Virgina, in 1938. They are still producing marbles. The company only produced swirls. In the early 1980s the company produced a series of marbles that are similar to two-color and three-color swirls produced during the 1930s. They also produced a marble that looks like a Wire Pull. These marbles are referred to as "New Old-Fashioneds". They are often mistaken for older swirls. You can tell the difference, because they have a very shiny or oily surface to them. Champion Agate also produced a short run of marbles about twenty years ago. These are very bright colors and are called furnace scraping marbles.

294. Champion Agate Company, Furnace Scraping. 5/8". $100.

295. Champion Agate Company, Furnace Scraping. 5/8". $75.

Champion Agate Furnace Scraping

Up to: 5/8"		9.9-9.7	9.6-9.3	9.2-9.0	8.9-8.5	8.4-8.0	7.9-7.0
	High	175.00	120.00	95.00	NA	NA	NA
	Low	5.00	4.00	2.00	NA	NA	NA
	Average	22.25	17.30	12.31	NA	NA	NA
	Quantity	25	14	17	0	0	0

296. Champion Agate Company, Swirl. 19/32". $10.

297. Champion Agate Company, Swirl. 5/8". $15.

Other Champion Agate Swirls

Up to:		9.9-9.7	9.6-9.3	9.2-9.0	8.9-8.5	8.4-8.0	7.9-7.0
5/8"	High	22.00	11.00	5.00	NA	NA	NA
	Low	1.00	2.00	1.00	NA	NA	NA
	Average	8.01	6.00	3.86	NA	NA	NA
	Quantity	27	8	11	0	0	0

HEATON AGATE COMPANY/ C.E. BOGARD & SONS/ THE BOGARD COMPANY/ JABO, INC./ JABO-VITRO AGATE, INC.

The Heaton Agate Company began operations in 1946 or 1947 in Pennsboro, West Virginia. It was originally run by Bill Heaton and Oris Hanlon. Hanlon left the company in 1947 to found the Cairo Novelty Company. Until the early 1960s, the company produced a variety of opaque swirls and transparent swirls, as well as cat's-eyes and game marbles. During the 1960s, production of swirls ceased and the company restricted itself to producing cat's-eyes and industrial marbles. It is reported that Heaton possessed a 3/8" marble making machine and produced 3/8" cat's-eyes. Specific types of swirls and cat's-eyes have still not been positively attributed to the company, but research continues in this area.

C.E. Bogard bought the Heaton Agate Company in 1971 and renamed it the C.E. Bogard & Sons Company. In 1983, the company name was changed to The Bogard Company by Clayton Bogard's son, Jack. Bogard produced a variety of cat's-eyes, clearies, and opaques. According to Jack Bogard, the company also produced an experimental marble (transparent clear base with interior green wisps) that can be found in the Mountaineer blister packs that the company marketed. None of Bogard's marbles have much value if they are not in their original packaging.

JABO, Inc., was organized in 1987 by Jack Bogard, Dave McCullough (who had spent many years at Champion Agate), and Joanne Argabrite. The machinery was moved to Reno, Ohio. The company produced industrial marbles, mainly opaques. However, Dave McCullough would produce three or four limited runs each year of "Classics" in sizes from 5/8" to 1". Each run was different from any previous run, and the marbles were not like any other company's. Many fluoresce and they contain many innovative colors and were produced in very short runs.

141

In early 1996, JABO, Inc. bought Vitro Agate Company, moving the Vitro machinery from Anacortes, Washington, to the Reno, Ohio, location. The JABO, Inc. was reorganized as JABO-Vitro Agate Company. The company now produces a wide variety of swirl marbles.

298. Heaton Agate Company, Swirl. 5/8". $5.

299. Heaton Agate Company, Swirl. 5/8". $5.

300. Heaton Agate Company, Swirl. 5/8". $5.

301. Heaton Agate Company, Swirl. 5/8". $5.

Heaton Agate Swirl

Up to: 5/8"		9.9-9.7	9.6-9.3	9.2-9.0	8.9-8.5	8.4-8.0	7.9-7.0
	High	11.00	NA	4.00	NA	NA	NA
	Low	5.00	NA	4.00	NA	NA	NA
	Average	7.00	NA	4.00	NA	NA	NA
	Quantity	6	0	1	0	0	0

CAIRO NOVELTY COMPANY

The Cairo Novelty Company began operations in 1948 in Cairo, West Virginia. With the financial backing of two local merchants (John Sandy and Dennis Farley), it had been formed late in the prior year by Oris Hanlon, who had left Heaton Agate Company. The company had only one marble machine, but a design innovation by Hanlon (which is patented) allowed it to produce marbles at a fifty percent faster rate than any other machine at the time. The company produced a wide variety of swirls, from peewee size to 3/4". Many of these marbles fluoresce. Their major account was Woolworth's, and they packaged mesh bags with the Woolworth's label on them. Cairo also marketed marbles in boxes with their own name. Both of these original packages are hard to find. The company also produced and marketed a game called "Trap the Fox" in the late 1940s. The game included black and white swirls (the hounds) and an opaque marble (the fox). A flash flood in 1950 seriously curtailed operations, but Cairo was able to produce marbles until 1953. More research needs to be done in order to identify the marbles that were specifically made by this plant.

302. Cairo Novelty Company, Swirl. 5/8". $2.

303. Cairo Novelty Company, Swirl. 5/8". $5.

Cairo Novelty Swirl

Up to:		9.9-9.7	9.6-9.3	9.2-9.0	8.9-8.5	8.4-8.0	7.9-7.0
5/8"	High	8.00	NA	NA	NA	NA	NA
	Low	0.50	NA	NA	NA	NA	NA
	Average	3.56	NA	NA	NA	NA	NA
	Quantity	12	0	0	0	0	0

DAVIS MARBLE WORKS

Wilson Davis founded The Davis Marble Works in 1947, in Pennsboro, West Virginia. He was a World War II veteran and purchased an old Alley Agate marble making machine from Corning Glass. Marbles were only produced for a short period of time. Davis produced transparent swirls.

305. Playrite Marble Company, Swirl. 19/32". $2 each.

304. Playrite Marble Company, Swirl. 19/32". $2 each.

Davis Marble Works Swirl

Up to:		9.9-9.7	9.6-9.3	9.2-9.0	8.9-8.5	8.4-8.0	7.9-7.0
5/8"	High	13.00	NA	NA	NA	NA	NA
	Low	0.75	NA	NA	NA	NA	NA
	Average	7.71	NA	NA	NA	NA	NA
	Quantity	16	0	0	0	0	0

JACKSON MARBLE COMPANY

Carol Jackson founded The Jackson Marble Company about 1945, near Pennsboro, West Virginia. He had previously been a machine operator at Champion Agate Company. The company only produced about two boxcars full of marbles. Jackson produced transparent swirls.

306. Jackson Marble Company, Swirl. 5/8". $10 each.

307. Jackson Marble Company, Swirl. 5/8". $10 each.

Jackson Marble Works Swirl

Up to:		9.9-9.7	9.6-9.3	9.2-9.0	8.9-8.5	8.4-8.0	7.9-7.0
5/8"	High	17.00	NA	NA	NA	NA	NA
	Low	1.00	NA	NA	NA	NA	NA
	Average	9.67	NA	NA	NA	NA	NA
	Quantity	6	0	0	0	0	0

VACOR DE MEXICO

Vacor de Mexico is a Mexican manufacturer of marbles. The company began operations sometime in the 1930s and today is one of the largest, if not the largest, manufacturer of marbles in the world. Their marbles are marketed under a variety of imaginative names: Pirate, Galaxy, Meteor, Galacticas, Silver, Agate. They are readily identifiable based on two features. First, the marbles tend to have an oily or iridescent sheen to them. Second, the glass tends to have ripples and creases in the surface. These marbles have little value to collectors. See pictures #308 and #309.

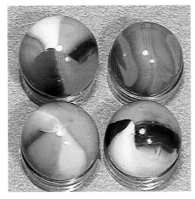

308. Vacor de Mexico,
Assorted. 5/8" & 7/8". $1.

309. Vacor de Mexico,
Assorted. 5/8". $0.25.

EUROPEAN MACHINE-MADE MARBLES

Machine-made marbles that were manufactured in Europe have begun to be identified by collectors. There are several types of marbles that have been positively identified as coming from Europe.

FOREIGN SPARKLER

The first is the "foreign sparkler." These have appeared in two versions. The faded pastel color, and a more colorful version. The faded pastel type appears to be of more recent vintage than the brighter type, and appears to have been made by a different manufacturer. The "bright" type has a thin vane in the center with assorted bright colors on it. The poles exhibit the "V" or "U" pattern similar to Master Marbles. These marbles are from the 1950s to the 1970s and were produced in Germany. Aside from loose examples, I have seen two examples, each embedded in a bar of soap shaped like a little girl. The "faded pastel" type has a wide vane that fills the marble. There may be oxblood in the core.

310. German, Foreign
Sparkler. 3/4". $5.

311. German, Foreign
Sparkler. 3/4". $5.

145

Foreign Sparkler

Up to:		9.9-9.7	9.6-9.3	9.2-9.0	8.9-8.5	8.4-8.0	7.9-7.0
5/8"	High	14.50	13.00	NA	NA	NA	NA
	Low	5.00	10.00	NA	NA	NA	NA
	Average	10.31	11.50	NA	NA	NA	NA
	Quantity	8	2	0	0	0	0
7/8"	High	29.00	14.00	27.00	NA	NA	NA
	Low	3.00	14.00	7.00	NA	NA	NA
	Average	14.17	14.00	12.00	NA	NA	NA
	Quantity	16	1	25	0	0	0

FOREIGN SWIRLS AND FOREIGN STRIPED TRANSPARENTS

There are two other types of marbles that were produced in Germany from the 1950s to the 1970s. One type is a swirl of one or two colors in white, similar in appearance to a Ravenswood Big Buddy. The other type is similar to a Christensen Agate striped transparent with white stripes in a transparent color.

312. German, Swirl. 7/8". $5 each.

313. German, Striped Transparent. 5/8" to 3/4". $1 to 10 each.

Foreign Swirls & Striped Transparents

Up to:		9.9-9.7	9.6-9.3	9.2-9.0	8.9-8.5	8.4-8.0	7.9-7.0
5/8"	High	9.00	2.00	NA	NA	NA	NA
	Low	1.00	1.00	NA	NA	NA	NA
	Average	2.23	1.50	NA	NA	NA	NA
	Quantity	16	2	0	0	0	0
3/4"	High	6.00	1.00	2.50	0.25	NA	NA
	Low	1.00	1.00	0.25	0.25	NA	NA
	Average	4.25	1.00	1.58	0.25	NA	NA
	Quantity	4	1	3	1	0	0
7/8"	High	41.00	5.00	3.00	NA	NA	NA
	Low	2.00	3.00	3.00	NA	NA	NA
	Average	11.08	4.00	3.00	NA	NA	NA
	Quantity	13	2	2	0	0	0

WIRE PULL

Another type of German marble is a Wire Pull. These have been found in a multitude of sizes, base colors, and wire colors. These were also produced from the 1950s to the 1970s.

314. German, Wire Pull. 7/8". $10.

315. German, Wire Pull. 7/8". $10.

German Wire Pull

Up to:		9.9-9.7	9.6-9.3	9.2-9.0	8.9-8.5	8.4-8.0	7.9-7.0
5/8"	High	5.00	NA	NA	NA	NA	NA
	Low	0.25	NA	NA	NA	NA	NA
	Average	1.65	NA	NA	NA	NA	NA
	Quantity	10	0	0	0	0	0
1"	High	17.00	7.00	4.00	NA	NA	NA
	Low	1.00	2.00	3.00	NA	NA	NA
	Average	6.43	4.66	3.50	NA	NA	NA
	Quantity	23	18	2	0	0	0

CZECHOSLOVAKIA

There are several types of marbles that are known to have been produced in Czechoslovakia, probably just prior to or just after World War II. One type looks like Guinea with a seam around the equator, and that has been lightly acid washed. A rarer Czechoslovakian machine made is also seamed and lightly acid washed. These have stripes of a color floating above a white core, or a banana-type cat's-eye. There is also a very small group of corkscrew-style marbles that were made in Czechoslovakia. This small group was found in Europe, and was probably manufactured in the 1930s. Some are a corkscrew type that is transparent clear on one side and transparent vaseline yellow on the other. The other is a corkscrew consisting of tiny pieces of colored glass (like Guinea flecks) in transparent clear.

316. Czechoslova-
kian, Zebra.
25/32". $75.

317. Czechoslova-
kian, Guinea.
21/32". $75.

Czechoslovakia Seamed

Up to: 7/8"		9.9-9.7	9.6-9.3	9.2-9.0	8.9-8.5	8.4-8.0	7.9-7.0
	High	80.00	NA	NA	NA	NA	NA
	Low	35.00	NA	NA	NA	NA	NA
	Average	66.67	NA	NA	NA	NA	NA
	Quantity	6	0	0	0	0	0

FOREIGN CAT'S-EYES

Virtually every manufacturer, since the late 1940s, has made cat's-eye marbles. The majority of cat's-eye marbles that you will find are foreign-made. Almost all of those have little value to collectors.

Cat's-eyes that can be identied as Peltier, Master, Marble King or Vitro Agate have been discussed in each of those sections. The table below covers other cat's-eyes (mostly foreign).

318. Cat's-eye.
5/8". $25.

319. Cat's-eye.
5/8". $0.1.

320. A432Cat's-
eye. 5/8". $0.1.

Foreign Cat's-eyes

Up to:		9.9-9.7	9.6-9.3	9.2-9.0	8.9-8.5	8.4-8.0	7.9-7.0
5/8"	High	26.00	8.00	NA	NA	NA	NA
	Low	0.01	0.25	NA	NA	NA	NA
	Average	7.32	4.08	NA	NA	NA	NA
	Quantity	10	3	0	0	0	0
3/4"	High	8.00	NA	NA	NA	NA	NA
	Low	2.00	NA	NA	NA	NA	NA
	Average	5.00	NA	NA	NA	NA	NA
	Quantity	2	0	0	0	0	0

OTHER MACHINE-MADE MARBLES

AVENTURINE

Aventurine is a metallic precipitate in the glass. It is found in virtually all types of marbles, but most notably in swirls and in cat's-eyes. The table below is for aventurine swirls. Cat's-eyes have been discussed under each company.

321. Unidentified West Virginia Company, Aventurine. 5/8". $15.

322. Unidentified West Virginia Company, Aventurine. 3/4". $40.

323. Unidentified West Virginia Company, Aventurine. 5/8". $25.

Aventurine Swirls

Up to:		9.9-9.7	9.6-9.3	9.2-9.0	8.9-8.5	8.4-8.0	7.9-7.0
5/8"	High	30.00	6.00	10.00	NA	NA	NA
	Low	6.00	6.00	6.00	NA	NA	NA
	Average	12.92	6.00	8.50	NA	NA	NA
	Quantity	13	1	4	0	0	0

METALLIC

Marbles with metallic stripes have been made by several manufacturers, including Alley Agate and Champion Agate. Usually, they have a silvery stripe on the colored swirl of a common swirl marble. Occasionally, you will find a silver stripe on a clearie or a copper colored stripe on a swirl.

324. Unidentified West Virginia Company, Metallic. 19/32". $10.

325. Unidentified West Virginia Company, Metallic. 5/8". $20.

Metallic Swirls and Stripes

Up to:		9.9-9.7	9.6-9.3	9.2-9.0	8.9-8.5	8.4-8.0	7.9-7.0
5/8"	High	17.00	13.00	15.00	NA	NA	NA
	Low	6.00	4.00	3.00	NA	NA	NA
	Average	11.67	8.50	4.00	NA	NA	NA
	Quantity	13	2	8	0	0	0

OTHER MACHINE-MADE PATCHES

Most of the companies produced patch marbles. The more readily identifiable ones have been discussed under each company. However, there are patches that cannot be identified to any specific company because machinery was sold from one company to the other, especially in West Virginia during the 1940s and 1950s.

326. Unidentified West Virginia Company, Patch. 9/16". $1.

327. Unidentified West Virginia Company, Patch. 5/8". $0.5.

Patch (unidentified manufacturer)

Up to:		9.9-9.7	9.6-9.3	9.2-9.0	8.9-8.5	8.4-8.0	7.9-7.0
5/8"	High	15.00	NA	NA	NA	NA	NA
	Low	0.01	NA	NA	NA	NA	NA
	Average	0.76	NA	NA	NA	NA	NA
	Quantity	27	0	0	0	0	0

OTHER MACHINE-MADE SWIRLS

Most of the companies produced swirl marbles. The more readily identifiable ones have been discussed under each company. However, there are swirls that cannot be identified to any specific company because machinery was sold from one company to the other, especially in West Virginia during the 1940s and 1950s.

328. Unidentified West Virginia Company, Swirl. 5/8".
$0.25 to 1.00 each.

329. Unidentified West Virginia Company, Swirl. 21/32". $15.

330. Unidentified West Virginia Company, Swirl. 11/16". $15.

331. Unidentified West Virginia Company, Swirl. 5/8". $0.5.

332. Unidentified West Virginia
Company, Swirl. 5/8". $10.

Swirl (unidentified manufacturer)

Up to: 5/8"		9.9-9.7	9.6-9.3	9.2-9.0	8.9-8.5	8.4-8.0	7.9-7.0
	High	22.00	NA	NA	NA	NA	NA
	Low	0.01	NA	NA	NA	NA	NA
	Average	1.83	NA	NA	NA	NA	NA
	Quantity	54	0	0	0	0	0

CONTEMPORARY HANDMADE MARBLES

Modern artists produce marbles in a variety of styles. They are produced as canes or one-offs, hot glass, and lampwork. The tables below are by artist. Many artists produce several different styles, however almost all artists confine themselves to a single technique. The tables below are not inclusive of all artists but represent marbles we have had in auction. They provide prices for undamaged marbles.

333. Contemporary Handmade,
Dan Ambrose. 5" high. $60.

Dan Ambrose

Up to:	High	Low	Average	Quantity
7/8"	32.00	19.00	22.50	6
1-1/4"	32.00	13.00	20.81	33

334. Contemporary Handmade,
Rob Livesey. 31/32". $20.

335. Contemporary Handmade,
Rob Livesey. 31/32". $20.

David Atkinson

Up to:	High	Low	Average	Quantity
1"	35.00	18.00	21.35	13
1-3/8"	24.00	24.00	24.00	1
2-1/4"	52.00	22.00	34.25	4

Geoffrey Beetem

Up to:	High	Low	Average	Quantity
1-1/4"	81.00	30.00	43.28	42
1-1/2"	82.00	22.00	44.20	115
1-3/4"	250.00	32.00	73.23	124
2"	280.00	75.00	144.75	12
2-1/2"	300.00	210.00	247.50	5

338. Contemporary Handmade,
Daniel Benway. 2-1/4". $200.

Daniel Benway

Up to:	High	Low	Average	Quantity
1"	20.00	17.00	19.00	3
1-1/4"	32.00	20.00	26.40	5

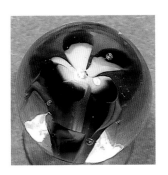

339. Contemporary
Handmade, Boyer
Glassworks. 1-1/4". $75.

340. Contemporary
Handmade, Boyer
Glassworks. 1-5/8". $75.

Boyer Glassworks

Up to:	High	Low	Average	Quantity
1-1/4"	30.00	17.00	24.66	3
2-1/4"	36.00	36.00	36.00	1

341. Contemporary
Handmade, Brookside
Glass. 1-5/8". $35.

342. Contemporary
Handmade, Brookside
Glass. 1-3/8". $30.

Brookside Glass

Up to: 1-1/2"	High 45.00	Low 20.00	Average 29.75	Quantity 80

344. Contemporary
Handmade, Robert
Brown. 25/32". $40.

Robert Brown

Up to: 1"	High 32.00	Low 10.00	Average 25.40	Quantity 8

345. Contemporary
Handmade, William
Burchfield. 7/8". $40.

346. Contemporary
Handmade, William
Burchfield. 7/8". $40.

William Burchfield

Up to:	High	Low	Average	Quantity
1"	75.00	36.00	52.39	5

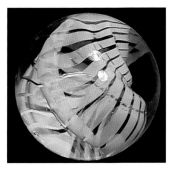 

347. Contemporary Hand-made, California Glass Studios. 1-3/4". $75.

348. Contemporary Hand-made, California Glass Studios. 1-3/4". $125.

California Glass Studios

Up to:	High	Low	Average	Quantity
1-7/8"	80.00	45.00	55.26	17
2-1/2"	75.00	75.00	75.00	1

349. Contemporary Handmade, Shane Caswell. 1-1/4". $30.

350. Contemporary Handmade, Shane Caswell. 1-1/2". $50.

Shane Caswell

Up to:	High	Low	Average	Quantity
1-1/2"	35.00	20.00	27.55	10
2-1/4"	110.00	32.00	42.33	6

351. Contemporary Handmade, Claystone Marbles. 3/4". $20.

352. Contemporary Handmade, Claystone Marbles. 3/4". $20.

Claystone Marbles

Up to:	High	Low	Average	Quantity
3/4"	14.00	7.00	9.11	18
1-1/4"	42.00	10.00	17.24	6

353. Contemporary Handmade, Gerry Colman. 7/8". $30.

354. Contemporary Handmade, Gerry Colman. 7/8". $75.

Gerry Colman

Up to:	High	Low	Average	Quantity
7/8"	75.00	30.00	45.33	9
1-1/4"	120.00	95.00	108.75	4
1-1/2"	150.00	32.00	95.36	11

355. Contemporary Handmade,
Francis Coupal. 1-3/4". $90.

356. Contemporary Handmade,
Francis Coupal. 1-3/4". $35.

Francis Coupal

Up to:	High	Low	Average	Quantity
1-1/4"	22.00	20.00	21.19	5
1-1/2"	70.00	22.00	37.55	36
1-3/4"	170.00	22.00	60.19	76
2"	125.00	40.00	69.50	14
2-1/2"	240.00	90.00	137.50	12

357. Contemporary Hand-
made, Crystal Myths. 2".
$100.

358. Contemporary Hand-
made, Crystal Myths. 1-3/4".
$80.

Crystal Myths

Up to:	High	Low	Average	Quantity
1"	48.00	8.00	20.83	6
1-1/2"	55.00	29.00	37.00	6
1-7/8"	100.00	46.00	75.33	3
2"	95.00	35.00	56.11	9

359. Contemporary Handmade,
Dale Danowski. 3/4". $20.

360. Contemporary Handmade,
Dale Danowski. 3/4". $20.

Dale Danowski

Up to:	High	Low	Average	Quantity
7/8"	39.00	8.00	14.28	87
1"	26.00	12.00	14.24	22

362. Contemporary Handmade,
Jim Davis. 1-1/2". $50.

361. Contemporary Handmade,
Jim Davis. 2". $75.

Jim Davis (Indiana)

Up to:	High	Low	Average	Quantity
1-1/2"	76.00	32.00	46.75	5

363. Contemporary Handmade, Davis Handmade Marbles. 1-7/16". $50.

364. Contemporary Handmade, Davis Handmade Marbles. 1-7/16". $50.

365. Contemporary Handmade, Davis Handmade Marbles. 1-9/16". $20.

366. Contemporary Handmade, Davis Handmade Marbles. 1-9/16". $20.

Davis Handmade Marbles

Up to:	High	Low	Average	Quantity
1"	23.00	10.00	14.66	9
1-3/8"	36.00	10.00	15.58	6
1-5/8"	75.00	8.00	16.53	731
2-1/4"	68.50	30.00	34.27	5

367. Contemporary Handmade, Davis Handmade Marbles. 1-9/16". $20.

Richard Federici

Up to:	High	Low	Average	Quantity
1-3/4"	31.00	31.00	31.00	1

368. Contemporary Handmade, Doug Ferguson. 15/16". $20.

369. Contemporary Handmade, Doug Ferguson. 15/16". $20.

Doug Ferguson

Up to:	High	Low	Average	Quantity
1"	35.00	14.00	21.72	14
1-1/4"	65.00	14.00	30.65	16
1-1/2"	110.00	22.00	48.28	14

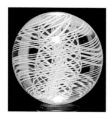

370. Contemporary Handmade, Jody Fine. 1-1/4". $20.

373. Contemporary Handmade, Jody Fine. 1-1/4". $75.

371. Contemporary Handmade, Jody Fine. 1-1/4". $20.

372. Contemporary Handmade, Jody Fine. 1". $17.5.

Jody Fine

Up to:	High	Low	Average	Quantity
7/8"	21.00	8.00	12.13	66
1"	27.50	10.00	14.38	42
1-1/4"	32.50	10.00	15.64	23
1-1/2"	37.50	13.00	20.16	15

374. Contemporary Handmade, Drew Fritts. 1-5/8". $125.

375. Contemporary Handmade, Drew Fritts. 1-5/8". $125.

Drew Fritts

Up to:	High	Low	Average	Quantity
1"	50.00	48.00	48.67	3
1-3/4"	185.00	55.00	85.07	52

376. Contemporary Handmade, Fulton-Parker Glass. 1-1/2". $60.

377. Contemporary Handmade, Fulton-Parker Glass. 2". $80.

Fulton-Parker Glass

Up to:	High	Low	Average	Quantity
7/8"	25.00	12.00	21.18	17
1-3/4"	27.00	27.00	27.00	2
2"	32.00	30.00	31.00	2

378. Contemporary Handmade, Gibson Glass. 2". $15.

379. Contemporary Handmade, Gibson Glass. 1-5/8". $12.5.

Gibson Glass

Up to:	High	Low	Average	Quantity
1-1/4"	24.00	9.00	15.61	13
1-1/2"	35.50	10.00	20.03	35
1-3/4"	26.00	10.00	19.94	19
2-1/4"	27.00	16.50	21.75	2

380. Contemporary Handmade, John Gilvey. 1-3/4". $300.

John Gilvey

Up to:	High	Low	Average	Quantity
1-7/8"	165.00	165.00	165.00	1

381. Contemporary Hand-
made, Greg Hoglin. 1". $40.

382. Contemporary Hand-
made, Greg Hoglin. 1-1/4". $50.

Greg Hoglin

Up to:	High	Low	Average	Quantity
7/8"	37.00	26.00	28.54	14
1-1/2"	65.00	32.00	39.88	6

383. Contemporary Handmade,
Sam Hogue. 1-5/8". $30.

384. Contemporary Handmade,
Sam Hogue. 1-1/2". $25.

Sam Hogue

Up to:	High	Low	Average	Quantity
1-1/2"	32.00	19.00	27.33	3
2"	36.00	22.00	34.50	5

385. Contemporary Handmade, Dinah Hulet. 7/8". $200.

386. Contemporary Handmade, Dinah Hulet. 1". $150.

Dinah Hulet

Up to:	High	Low	Average	Quantity
1"	150.00	70.00	98.33	6
1-1/4"	195.00	75.00	127.50	5

389. Contemporary Handmade, Lundberg Studios. 2". $300.

390. Contemporary Handmade, Lundberg Studios. 1-3/4". $200.

Lundberg Studios

Up to:	High	Low	Average	Quantity
1-3/4"	150.00	110.00	130.00	2
2-1/2"	250.00	250.00	250.00	1

391. Contemporary Handmade, Nadine Macdonald. 1-1/8". $25.

392. Contemporary Handmade, Nadine Macdonald. 7/8". $15.

393. Contemporary Handmade, Nadine Macdonald. 1". $25.

394. Contemporary Handmade, Nadine Macdonald. 7/8". $15.

Nadine Macdonald

Up to:	High	Low	Average	Quantity
5/8"	12.00	5.00	7.13	27
7/8"	17.00	8.00	10.54	36
1"	32.00	10.00	14.24	15

395. Contemporary Handmade, Steve Maslach. 1". $20.

396. Contemporary Handmade, Steve Maslach. 7/8". $15.

Steve Maslach

Up to:	High	Low	Average	Quantity
7/8"	19.00	7.00	11.88	30
1"	24.50	10.00	13.44	8
1-1/4"	20.50	10.00	14.66	3
1-1/2"	31.50	12.00	17.90	10

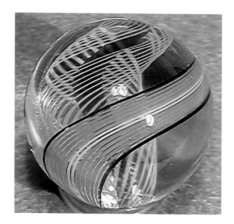

397. Contemporary Handmade, Steve Maslach. 7/8". $15.

398. Contemporary Handmade, Steve Maslach. 7/8". $15.

Don Mathis

Up to:	High	Low	Average	Quantity
7/8"	22.00	8.00	13.50	4
1-1/4"	19.00	8.00	13.17	9

399. Contemporary Handmade, Boyd A. Miller. 1-5/8". $30.

400. Contemporary Handmade, Boyd A. Miller. 1-1/2". $30.

Boyd A. Miller

Up to:	High	Low	Average	Quantity
7/8"	18.50	12.00	15.40	10
1-1/2"	40.00	17.00	25.08	47
1-3/4"	46.50	18.50	29.29	40

401. Contemporary
Handmade, John
Hamon Miller.
1-3/8". $30.

402. Contemporary
Handmade, John
Hamon Miller.
1-1/4". $25.

403. Contemporary
Handmade, John
Hamon Miller.
1". $20.

John Hamon Miller

Up to:	High	Low	Average	Quantity
5/8"	19.00	5.00	13.00	10
7/8"	35.00	9.00	17.50	28
1-1/4"	34.00	13.00	20.25	75
1-1/2"	45.00	15.00	26.77	24

404. Contemporary
Handmade, Murray's
Modern Marbles.
1-1/8". $30.

405. Contemporary
Handmade, Murray's
Modern Marbles.
1-3/8". $30.

406. Contemporary
Handmade, Murray's
Modern Marbles.
1-3/4". $250.

William F. Murray

Up to:	High	Low	Average	Quantity
1-1/4"	36.00	19.00	26.00	12
1-1/2"	36.00	22.00	29.00	10
2-1/4"	50.00	32.00	39.66	3

Frank Oddu

Up to:	High	Low	Average	Quantity
1"	40.00	17.00	20.37	16
1-1/4"	34.00	19.00	22.50	6
1-1/2"	28.00	20.00	23.62	4

409. Contemporary Handmade, George O'Grady. 1-1/4". $45.

410. Contemporary Handmade, George O'Grady. 1-1/4". $45.

George O'Grady

Up to:	High	Low	Average	Quantity
1"	24.00	22.00	23.00	2
1-1/4"	60.00	29.00	38.00	5
1-1/2"	65.00	40.00	51.66	3
1-3/4"	95.00	56.00	73.20	5

411. Contemporary Handmade, Jerry Park. 15/16". $15.

412. Contemporary Handmade, Jerry Park. 15/16". $15.

Jerry Park

Up to:	High	Low	Average	Quantity
1"	26.00	12.00	13.43	11
1-1/4"	44.00	10.00	15.55	25
1-1/2"	76.00	12.00	16.87	34

413. Contemporary Handmade, Scott Patrick. 3/4". $50.

414. Contemporary Handmade, Scott Patrick. 5/8"-23/32". $10 to 20 each.

Scott Patrick

Up to:	High	Low	Average	Quantity
3/4"	40.00	8.00	12.33	18
1-1/4"	75.00	22.00	32.53	8

415. Contemporary Handmade, George Pavliscak. 1-1/4". $35.

416. Contemporary Handmade, George Pavliscak. 15/16". $25.

George Pavliscak

Up to:	High	Low	Average	Quantity
1-1/4"	50.00	23.00	27.93	8

417. Contemporary Handmade, Gregg Pessman. 1-1/8". $50.

418. Contemporary Handmade, Gregg Pessman. 1-1/8". $50.

419. Contemporary Handmade, Gregg Pessman. 1-1/8". $50.

420. Contemporary Handmade, Gregg Pessman. 1-1/8". $45.

Gregg Pessman

Up to:	High	Low	Average	Quantity
1-1/4"	32.00	19.00	26.58	12
1-1/2"	70.00	38.00	50.25	52

421. Contemporary Handmade, Chuck Pound. 1-1/8". $40.

422. Contemporary Handmade, Chuck Pound. 1-1/4". $60.

Chuck Pound

Up to:	High	Low	Average	Quantity
1-3/8"	75.00	49.00	57.40	5
1-1/2"	100.00	32.00	58.46	7

423. Contemporary Hand-
made, Cathy Richardson.
1-3/4". $250.

424. Contemporary
Handmade, Cathy
Richardson. 1-5/8". $225.

Cathy Richardson

Up to:	High	Low	Average	Quantity
1-3/8"	81.00	21.00	36.33	15
1-1/2"	120.00	45.00	70.0	5
2-1/4"	200.00	170.00	183.33	3
3"	265.00	265.00	265.00	1

425. Contemporary Hand-
made, Chris Robinson. 27/32".
$25.

426. Contemporary Hand-
made, Chris Robinson. 27/32".
$25.

Chris Robinson

Up to:	High	Low	Average	Quantity
7/8"	30.00	12.00	24.94	18

427. Contemporary Handmade, Salazar Art Glass. 1-1/2". $125.

428. Contemporary Handmade, Salazar Art Glass. 1-1/2". $125.

429. Contemporary Handmade, Salazar Art Glass. 1-3/8". $90.

430. Contemporary Handmade, Salazar Art Glass. 1-1/2". $125.

David Salazar

Up to:	High	Low	Average	Quantity
1"	65.00	14.00	32.67	18
1-5/8"	125.00	70.00	95.58	14
2"	155.00	75.00	106.67	6

431. Contemporary Handmade, Eddie Seese. 1-1/4". $30.

432. Contemporary Handmade, Eddie Seese. 1-1/4". $30.

433. Contemporary Handmade, Eddie Seese. 1-1/4". $30.

434. Contemporary Handmade, Eddie Seese. 1-3/8". $35.

Eddie Seese

Up to:	High	Low	Average	Quantity
1"	28.50	13.00	19.70	1
1-1/4"	43.00	17.00	28.94	33
1-1/2"	130.00	17.00	34.55	49
1-3/4"	71.00	48.00	59.50	2
2"	75.00	40.00	48.32	6

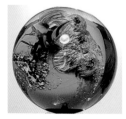

435. Contemporary Handmade, Josh Simpson. 1-1/12". $60.

436. Contemporary Handmade, Josh Simpson. 1-1/12". $125.

Josh Simpson

Up to:	High	Low	Average	Quantity
1-5/8"	95.00	50.00	73.25	8
2"	130.00	65.00	88.48	12

437. Contemporary Hand-made, Joe St. Clair. 1-1/12". $250.

438. Contemporary Hand-made, Joe St. Clair. 1-1/12". $250.

Joe St. Clair

Up to:	High	Low	Average	Quantity
1-3/4"	180.00	75.00	126.25	4
2-1/4"	100.00	85.00	92.50	2

439. Contemporary Handmade, Doug Sweet. 1-3/8". $90.

440. Contemporary Handmade, Doug Sweet. 1-1/2". $100.

Doug Sweet

Up to:	High	Low	Average	Quantity
1-3/4"	95.00	65.00	75.67	6
2-1/4"	120.00	75.00	93.33	3

441. Contemporary
Handmade, Jesse Taj.
1-1/2". $135.

Jesse Taj

Up to:	High	Low	Average	Quantity
1-1/2"	120.00	100.00	110.00	2

442. Contemporary
Handmade, Tom
Thornburgh. 1". $15.

443. Contemporary
Handmade, Tom
Thornburgh. 1". $25.

Tom Thornburgh

Up to:	High	Low	Average	Quantity
3/4"	11.00	5.00	8.54	15
1"	15.00	7.50	11.26	30

444. Contemporary
Handmade, Bruce
Troeh. 1-1/4". $50.

445. Contemporary
Handmade, Bruce
Troeh. 15/16". $20.

Bruce Troeh

Up to:	High	Low	Average	Quantity
5/8"	20.00	5.00	13.33	3
1"	60.00	19.00	33.40	5
1-1/4"	75.00	15.00	35.41	36
1-1/2"	80.00	55.00	67.50	2

446. Contemporary Handmade, Vermont Glass. 1-1/4". $25.

447. Contemporary Handmade, Vermont Glass. 1-3/8". $30.

448. Contemporary Handmade, Vermont Glass. 1-1/8". $25.

449. Contemporary Handmade, Vermont Glass. 1-3/4". $250.

Vermont Glass

Up to:	High	Low	Average	Quantity
1-1/4"	36.00	22.00	27.56	14
1-3/4"	55.00	28.00	36.55	18

450. Contemporary Handmade, Rolf & Genie Wald. 1". $30.

451. Contemporary Handmade, Rolf & Genie Wald. 1-1/4". $125.

452. Contemporary Handmade, Rolf & Genie Wald. 1". $35.

453. Contemporary Handmade, Rolf & Genie Wald. 1". $30.

Rolf & Genie Wald

Up to:	High	Low	Average	Quantity
7/8"	45.00	22.00	26.48	17
1-1/4"	60.00	25.00	31.68	12
1-1/2"	70.00	28.00	49.67	6

MARBLES IN ORIGINAL PACKAGING

454.
Cartoon Box
with Clay
marbles.
$125.

457. Original Box of Clays
(Germany). $75.

455. Reverse of #454.

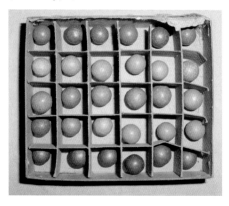

458. Interior of #457.

456. Original Box of Benningtons
(Germany). $100.

459. Mesh Bags of Clay
Marbles (France). $75.

460. Mosaic Game with Clay marbles (England). $50.

463. Marble Muggins Game with Clay marbles (damaged). $45.

461. Whirl-It game with Clay marbles (Germany). $100.

462. Interior of #461.

464. Interior of #463.

465. Original Mesh Bag with Handmade Opaques (Germany). $125.

468. Interior of #467.

466. Christensen Agate Company Favorites Box with Clay and Slag marbles. $500.

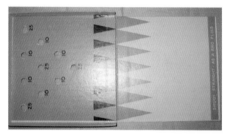

469. Interior of #467.

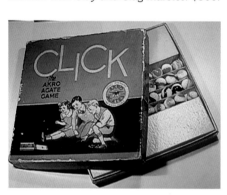

467. Akro Agate Company Click Game. $450.

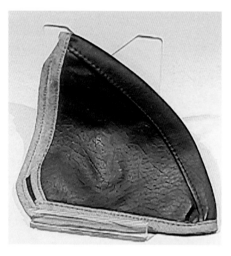

470. Akro Agate Company Kneepad. $125.

471. Reverse of #470.

472. Akro Agate Company No. 16 Sleeve with Slag marbles. $90.

473. Akro Agate Company No. 32 Sleeve with Corkscrews. $150.

474. Akro Agate Company Box from Gift Set with Slags. $300.

475. Akro Agate Company No. 0 Cardinal Red box. $400.

476. Akro Agate Company early No. 250 box with Popeyes. $2000.

477. Akro Agate Company No. 230 box. $350.

478. Akro Agate Company No. 250 box. $500.

479. Interior of #478.

480. Akro Agate Company
No. 300 box. $850.

484. Interior of #483.

481. Interior of #480.

482. Akro Agate Company
No. 200 tin. $1250.

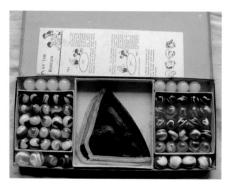

483. Interior of #482.

485. Interior of #483.

486. Akro Agate Company Gift Set (some marbles are not original). $500.

490. Interior of #489.

487. Akro Agate Company Gift Set. $1000.

491. Akro Agate Company No.1 Prize Name stock box. $1250.

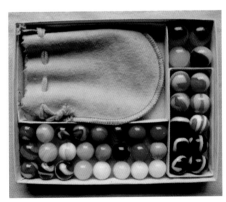

488. Interior of #487.

489. Akro Agate Company No. 1 Royals stock box (early). $600.

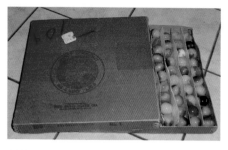

492. Akro Agate Company No. 1 Tricolor Agate stock box. $300.

495. Akro Agate Company Opaques stock box (early). $250.

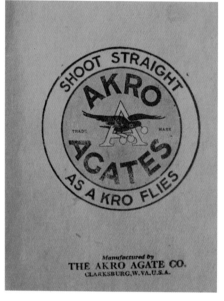

493. Akro Agate Company No. 2 Clearies stock box. $400.

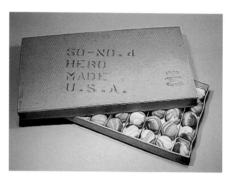

496. Akro Agate Company No. 4 Heros stock box. $2500.

494. Interior of #493.

497. Akro Agate Company Popeye box. $1200.

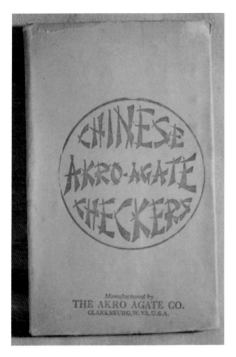

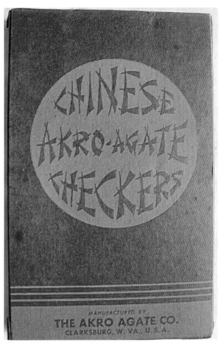

498. Akro Agate Company
Game Marbles box (tan). $25.

500. Akro Agate Company Game
Marbles box (red). $45.

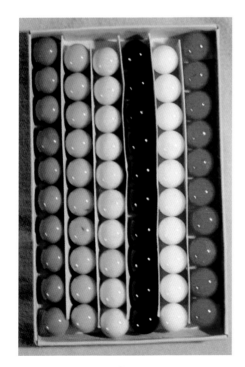

499. Interior of #498.

501. Interior of #500.

502. Akro Agate Company mesh bag (Royals). $100.

503. Akro Agate Company mesh bag (corkscrews). $100.

504. Akro Agate Company Solitary Checkers game. $30.

505. Interior of #504.

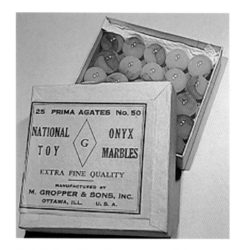

506. Peltier Glass Company stock box (Honey Onyx) (box is vintage to marbles, but not original to them). $2000.

507. Peltier Glass Company No. 106 Rainbo box. $150.

508. Master Marble Company
Sunbeam box. $400.

512. Master Marble Company Century of
Progress College Collection. $1,000.

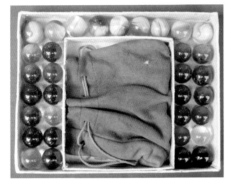

509. Interior of #508.

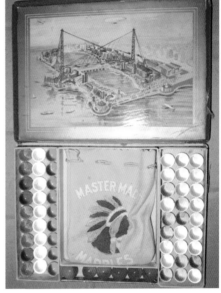

513. Interior of #510.

510. Master Marble Company Clearies
store display box. $200.

511. Master
Marble Company
Comets store
display box. $350.

514. Master Marble Company Century of Progress gift set (medium). $750.

517. Master Glass Company No. 10 box (clearies). $75.

515. Interior of #514.

518. Master Glass Company No. 13 box (clearies). $40.

519. Vitro Agate Company Salesman Sample box. $2500.

516. Master Marble Company mesh bag (Comets and Opaques). $100.

520. Interior of #519.

521. Interior of #519.

522. Interior of #519.

526. Vitro Agate Company
Conquerors mesh bag. $40.

523. Interior of #519.

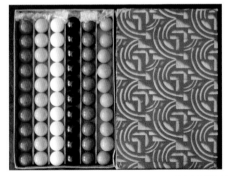

524. Vitro Agate Company
Opaques in Stained Glass
box. $150.

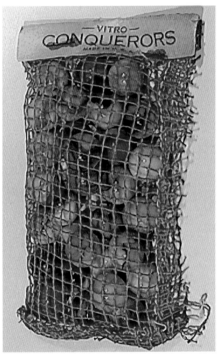

527. Vitro Agate Company
Conquerors mesh bag. $40.

525. Vitro Agate Company
box (Conquerors). $150.

528. Vitro Agate Company
Blackies poly bag. $35.

529. Vitro Agate Company
Tigereyes poly bag. $30.

530. Berry Pink
Game Marbles
box. $40.

531. Interior of #530.

532. Berry Pink Game Marbles box. $40.

533. Interior of #532.

534. Marble King Premium
mesh bag (Morton's Salt)
(Peltier Rainbos). $35.

535. Marble King Premium mesh bag
(Morton's Salt) (Peltier Rainbos). $35.

536. Marble King Rainbows poly
bag (Salesman Sample). $75.

537. Reverse of #536.

538. Marble King premium poly
bag (Nestle's) (Rainbows). $35.

539. Kayson's Marbles box
(West Virginia swirls). $75.

540. Norland
Marbles box
(West Virginia
swirls). $60.

541. Original box with German swirls (England). $75.

542. Shackman box (cat's-eyes). $25.

543. Interior of #542.

544. Allies sleeve with Alley swirls. $40.

545. Star Chinese checkers box. $80.

546. Bogard Mountaineer Shooters blister card. $30.

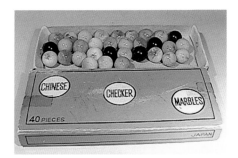

547. Chinese Checkers box (Japan). $40.

548. Stock box (West Virginia swirls). $150.

550. Jobber box (West Virginia swirls). $30.

549. Jobber box (West Virginia swirls). $20.

551. Jabo-Vitro Agate Classics box. $50.

552. Ravenswood Big Buddy mesh bag. $75.

553. Pressman mesh bag (Heaton Agate swirls). $40.

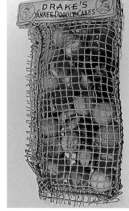

555. Advertising mesh bag (Drake's) (Peltier Rainbos). $40.

554. Pressman poly bag (Vitro Agate Conquerors). $30.

556. Advertising mesh bag (Starkey's) (Peltier Rainbos). $40.

557. Peltier Cat's-eye poly bag. $15.

558. Marble King Premium poly bag. $25.

559. Fantasy poly bag (modern Marble King Rainbos). $5.

One of the hottest areas of recent interest in marble collecting has been marbles in their original packaging. This is usually limited to machine-made marbles, however, you can find some handmade and non-glass marbles in their original packaging too.

Original packaging serves a very important purpose in the research of marble history. Almost all handmade marbles were sold in bulk, out of bins or large crates. This makes it almost impossible to construct a history of handmade marble manufacturing, or even to identify the country of origin of almost all handmade marbles. Machine-made marbles, on the other hand, were almost always sold in some sort of packaging. This is as much a reflection on the American predilection with marketing as it is on the distribution requirements of the marble manufacturers. As a result, almost every single type of machine-made marble exists in some form of original packaging, making the task of identifying machine-made marbles by manufacturer and date of manufacture fairly easy.

Original packaging can take a number of different forms. These include cardboard boxes, muslin bags, tin boxes, net or mesh bags, cellophane bags, polyvinyl bags, and blister cards.

The value of an original package of marbles is determined by a number of factors, including rarity of the package, condition of the package, condition of non-marble items in the package, rarity of the marbles, and condition of the marbles. Many types of marbles that are not valuable individually are very valuable when part of a package. This is because the packaging itself is very rare. Many marbles were distributed to retailers in bulk packaging. This bulk packaging (stock boxes, cartons, etc.) can also be very rare.

The condition of the packaging itself is the second most important determinant of value (after rarity of the package). Rips, tears, burst corners, water stains, rusting, tape tears, or scribbling on the package by an earlier owner, all depreciate the value of the packaging.

In many cases, packaging came with ancillary items: Kneepads, marble game instructions, contest cards. These items can greatly enhance the value of the original packaging.

Handmade or non-glass marbles in their original packages are fairly rare. These usually are cardboard boxes of sulphides, swirls, benningtons, clays or chinas, or muslin bags of clays.

Original packaging containing machine-made marbles is much more plentiful.

Marble Related Items

560. Mar-Bo-Gun on original card. $20.

195

561. Marx Skill Ball Game. $30.

564. Golden Rule Marble with original box and paperwork. $35.

562. Fisher Jewel Tray. $25.

565. Golden Rule Marble. $10.

563. Fisher Jewel Tray - NY World's Fair. $75.

566. Marble King leather pouch. $35.

567. Solitaire game. $60.

568. Interior of #567.

569. Tournament Pin. $100.

570. Tournament Pin. $100.

571. Tournament Pin. $45.

572. Tournament Pin. $75.

573. Tournament Pin. $60.

574. Tournament Pin. $75.

576. Tournament Medal. $250.

577. Tournament Medal. $250.

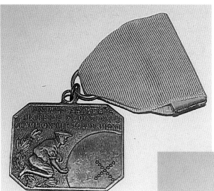

575. Tournament
Medal. $300.

578. Tournament
Medal. $250.

198

579. Tournament Ribbon (Press pass). $150.

580. Tournament Trophy. $600.

581. Tournament Trophy. $300.

582. Porcelain Bowl (England). $750.

583. Porcelain Tea Bowl (England). $500.

584. Porcelain Plate (England). $300.

586. Reverse of #585.

585. Lusterware Creamer
(England). $1000.

REPRODUCTIONS, FAKES, FANTASIES, & REPAIRED MARBLES

As with any collectible today, you should be aware that there are reproductions, fakes, fantasies, and repaired marbles out there. Reproduction of marble types is not a new phenomena. In fact, several of the early American marble companies attempted to produce machine-made marbles that reproduced handmade marbles. Sparklers and Sunbursts were an attempt to mimic onionskins; cat's-eyes were an attempt to mimic swirls; Bricks, slags and Akro Carnelian Agates and 'Ades were an attempt to mimic hand cut stones. All of these marbles, with the exception of the cat's-eyes perhaps, are highly collectible today.

As modern glass craftsmen began to produce contemporary handmade marbles a decade and a half ago, they naturally turned to antique handmade marbles as a guide. The Marble Collectors Society of America has been at the forefront of convincing many contemporary artisans to sign their marbles. This serves a two-fold purpose: A signed marble is not mistaken for an antique, and someday, when the marble does become an antique, the maker can still be recognized for his work. There are only a couple of contemporary artisans who still do not sign their works, but the number is much fewer than even five years ago. Unsigned contemporary handmade marbles can be identified by several features. First, the glass tends to be much clearer than you see in antique marbles. Old glass tends to have at least some tiny air bubbles in it. Contemporary marbles usually do not have tiny air bubbles in them that are not part of the design. Second, contemporary marbles usually have colors that you do not see in antique marbles. The colors tend to be much brighter than old colors. Third, contemporary marbles have a very smooth surface. Antique marbles almost always have ripples and creases running around the circumference of the marble in the glass, no matter how tiny those marks may be. Generally, the surface of contemporary marbles is much smoother and more even than antique marbles. Finally, contemporary marbles almost always do not have a pontil or the pontil is fire-polished. Antique marbles always have a pontil, although it may be ground. A modern artisan takes much more time with his marbles than the old craftsmen. Even if the pontils of an old marble were smoothed, it was usually done in a rush.

Peltier Glass Company comics have been reproduced for at least the past fifteen years. The original comics were made by a process that applied and fired a graphite image to the surface of a Peltier Peerless Patch. The marbles were always 19/32" to 11/16" in diameter and the transfers were always black (except for a couple of extremely rare experimentals). The reproductions that I have seen are of several different types. The twelve original comic characters (as well as the Cotes and Tom Mix) have been reproduced on Peltier Peerless Patches. However, the images have either been painted on, silk-screened on or applied as a decal. In all cases, if you rub your finger over the transfer, you can feel that it is on top of the marble surface. You cannot feel the transfer on an original comic because it was fired onto the marble. I have also seen reproduction comics on Marble King or Vitro Agate patch & ribbon marbles. Finally, I have seen reproduction comics on marbles larger than 11/16". There are also some reproduction comic marbles that have transfers of images that were never on the originals. These include Popeye and Jeff (of Mutt and Jeff). Usually, these are multicolor, which the original Peltier comics are not. Also, a firm by the name of Qualatex made a large number of advertising marbles during the 1970s and 1980s. These have a multitude of single color and multicolor images on them. They are not Peltier comics.

The recent explosion of interest in machine-made marbles has produced a new type of glassworker. These glassworkers, and there are only a few at this time, are making marbles that mimic machine-made marbles. They sometimes do this with glass from old marbles or cullet (re-works), and sometimes from new glass (reproductions). These glassworkers have resisted all attempts to convince them to sign their marbles. Some of their new designs are virtually indistinguishable from the original marbles to all but the most advanced collector. Among the marbles that these glassworkers have been reproducing are Leighton transitionals (transitionals with oxblood), rare and hybrid oxbloods, large slags, Christensen Agate Guineas and swirls, and Peltier National Line Rainbos. You must be very careful when buying these types of marbles.

Reworked marbles are marbles that are made from pieces of original marbles, cullet glass or a combination with new glass. Most of the reworked marbles that I have seen are reworked Leighton transitionals, Bricks, and oxbloods. These marbles are generally made by a process that melts or layers colors together or on top of one another. Most of these have been ground and polished. This is necessary because the process of making them does not create a smooth surface. Therefore, you can see grinding and polishing marks on each of the marble surfaces, especially if viewed under a 10x lens. Also, the polishing exposes air holes that were lying just beneath the surface. These air holes do not have melted edges, but rather have sharp edges that resulted from the polishing. For those reworked marbles that have not been ground or polished, the ones that I have seen have short, melted pontils or else have been fire polished. The surface is not completely smooth, but has melted ripples on it. Some early examples had vastly different colors of glass in them or had tiny copper pieces embedded in them. Be very aware of reworked marbles. None are signed.

Reproduction marbles are contemporary marbles that are made to duplicate as closely as possible the design and coloring of an original marble. I have seen examples of reproduction indians, lutzes, slags, Christensen Agate Guineas and swirls, and Peltier Tri-color National line Rainbos. Reproduction marbles are usually identifiable by a few factors. First, they tend to be the rarer examples. No one is going to take the time to reproduce a $10 or $15 marble, if they can reproduce a $100 or $300 marble with the same effort. Second, they don't look quite right. Trust your intuition. Third, antique handmade marbles always have tiny creases in the glass that resulted from their manufacture. Fourth, look at the pontils and see if they look right. On the other hand, machine-made marbles are a little more difficult. Remember, all machine-made marbles were made by machine (by definition). All reproduction marbles are made by hand. Look very, very closely at the surface. Does it look like it was made by a machine or was it hand-polished or fire polished in some way?

This brings up the topic of repaired marbles (including polished marbles). Polished and buffed marbles are readily identifiable with a little studying. There is no reason to polish or buff a marble, except to remove damage and enhance its collectibility. Handmade marbles should have pontils. Also, handmade marbles always have tiny creases on the surface that are removed by buffing. Look at the chips that remain and see if they have sharp or rounded edges. Rounded edges are usually a sign of buffing. Polished machine-made marbles are a little harder to detect. Almost all machine-made marbles have a very thin layer of surface glass that is removed by buffing. This removal exposes tiny air bubbles on the surface. If you look at these air bubbles and they have polishing grit in them, or the edges are not melted, then the marble has probably been buffed.

Some handmade marbles that have fractures can also be repaired. This is done by reheating the marble. This reheating usually destroys the tiny creases on the surface and also occasionally results in cloudiness in the marble.

Fantasies are items that never existed in original form. Examples of these are a recent glut of polyvinyl bags with old looking labels on them. For example, all of the Alox Manufacturing "Army," "Navy," and "Air Force" bags are fantasies, as well as a number of "gasoline station" and "beverage" bags. When looking at polyvinyl bags you should pay close attention to the marbles in them (many polyvinyl bags have modern marbles in them), the cardboard used for the label (does it look and smell old) and the staples used (most old staples are square in profile and will not be shiny).

In conclusion, follow these simple rules of collecting:

1. Get a money-back guarantee as to the authenticity of anything that you buy. If the seller won't guarantee the authenticity of what they are selling, buy from someone else.
2. Study your field. There is no substitute for knowledge and hands-on experience. Everyone makes mistakes, but you make less of them if you know what you are looking at.
3. Keep informed of new finds, rediscoveries, and news. Subscribe to one or more of the many newsletters or clubs. *Marble Mania®* has a quarterly column on new reproductions. The Marble Collectors Corner web site (www.blocksite.com) maintains an up-to-date list of reproductions, fakes, and fantasies, including images.
4. Try to attend meets or shows. You can learn more in one weekend of handling items than by reading all of the books in print.
5. When buying collectibles, only buy items that appeal to you. Don't buy something because you think that it is a good investment or because someone tells you that it is a good buy. Buy it because you like it. If you aren't willing to display it, don't buy it.
6. Don't ever buy on impulse. Carefully study everything that you are thinking of buying.
7. Buy the best that you can with your money. Use your precious funds to buy the best SINGLE item, not two or more lesser items. Your collection will be better for it.

GLOSSARY

AGGIE - a shooter made from the mineral agate.

ALLIES - derived from alleytors; prized shooters made of semiprecious minerals.

ANNEAL - to gradually reduce glass temperature in an oven or Lehr, so as to inhibit cracking in glass.

AVENTURINE - a type of glass containing particles of either copper (goldstone), chromic oxide (green aventurine) or ferric oxide (red aventurine), giving glass a glittering or shimmering appearance.

CANE - a long glass rod constructed of layers of different colors.

CHALKIES - unglazed marbles made from clay, limestone or gypsum.

CHIP - the spot where a piece has broken off the surface of a marble, usually from being hit. Small chips are sometimes called "flakes." A barely visible chip is sometimes called a "pinprick" or "pinpoint."

CLAMBROTH - milk glass marbles in solid color having many thin outer swirl lines of a different color or colors running from pontil to pontil.

CLAY - marbles made of clay, which may or may not be colored or glazed.

CLEARIE - clear glass marbles made in a variety of single colors.

CLOUD - an end of day marble where the colored flecks of glass in the marble are not stretched, such that they resemble clouds floating above the core.

COMIC - marbles manufactured by the Peltier Glass Company from 1928 through 1934. They have one of twelve different comic characters stamped and fired onto the marble, such that the transfer is permanent. May also have a transfer of Tom Mix or Cotes Bakery.

COMMIES - playing marbles made out of clay.

CONTEMPORARY GLASS - a marble handmade by a modern craftsman.

CRYSTAL - very clear, colorless glass.

CULLET - pieces of broken glass that are to be added to a batch.

DIAMETER - the length of a straight line through the center of a sphere. The size of a marble is measured by its diameter.

DING - the mark left on the surface of the marble by a small blow. The glass on the area damaged is still intact (unlike a chip). This mark is sometimes called a "moon," "subsurface moon" or "bruise."

DIVIDED CORE - swirl-type glass marble having colored bands in the center running from pontil to pontil.

END-OF-CANE - a handmade marble that was the first (start-of-cane) or final (last-of-cane) one produced from a cane. These are identifiable as marbles where the internal design ends before one of the pontil marks.

END OF DAY - a handmade glass marble that contains small stretched or unstretched flecks of colored glass that do not run continuously unbroken from pontil to pontil.

FRACTURE - an internal stress line caused by a blow to the surface, chemical stress or thermal stress to the glass. This term also refers to a hairline crack in a sulphide figure caused during manufacture.

FREESE IMPROVEMENT - modification made to Akro Agate machinery that eliminated tiny seam at either end of a machine-made marble and made them smoother. Involved off-setting the rollers on the marble-making machine. Named after an Akro employee and implemented around 1927.

FURNACE - a pot, day tank or continuous tank fabricated for melting glass.

GATHER - a portion of molten glass on a punty, sometimes called a glob.

HANDMADE - marbles that are made without the use of machines. There usually are cut-off marks (pontil marks) on one or both poles of the marble. A handmade glass marble is made by twisting glass off the end of a glass cane or by gathering glass on the end of a metal rod (punty).

IMMIE - a glass marble streaked with color.

INDIAN - handmade marble consisting of dark base glass with colorful bands applied in the surface or on top of it from pontil to pontil.

LATTICINIO - a swirl-type glass marble with thin strands in the center running from pontil to pontil that form a net when the marble was twisted.

LEHR - an annealing furnace or oven.

LUTZ - handmade glass marbles that contain finely ground goldstone.

MACHINE-MADE - a marble that is made by machines. Generally, they are perfectly round and have no pontil marks. These marbles were made after 1900, predominately in the United States.

MANUFACTURING DEFECT - a fold, crease, additional melted glass or open air bubble on the surface of a marble, or a hairline fracture in sulphide figures.

MIBS - the game of marbles, from a shortening of the word marbles.

MICA - mineral silicates that occur in thin sheets and are reflective or silvery in appearance. Coarsely ground flakes of mica are sometimes placed in handmade marbles.

MILKIES - translucent white glassies.

ONIONSKIN - an end of day marble where the colored flecks of glass are stretched, such that the core resembles the skin of an onion.

OPAQUE - a handmade or machine-made marble that is a single color and that is so dark that light does not shine through it.

PEE WEE - a marble that is 1/2" or less in diameter.

PEPPERMINT - a handmade swirl marble that has bands of red, white, and blue under the surface.

POLISHED - work which has been done to the surface of a marble to make it more presentable by clearing up cloudiness, surface roughness, scratches or small chips. A polished handmade marble no longer has pontils. A polished machine-made marble is missing the top layer of glass. A handmade marble that has been polished, but that still has its pontils is referred to as "buffed." A machine-made marble that still retains some of its original surface is also referred to by the same name.

PONTIL - a rough mark left on the pole of a marble where it was sheared off a rod or the end of a punty.

PUNTY - a long solid metal rod used to hold a glass object that is being made.

PURIE - a small, brightly colored Clearie.

RIBBON CORE - a handmade swirl with a single or two flat bands in the center running from pontil to pontil.

SHOOTER - the marble used to aim at and strike other marbles in a game. Regulation size is 1/2" to 3/4".

SINGLE GATHER - a marble that was made completely on the end of a punty and not from a cane.

SINGLE PONTIL - a marble with only one pontil, created from either the end of cane or single gathered.

SLAG - a marble made from two different colors of glass that were melted together in the same furnace pot. Due to the differing densities of the glass, they would not melt into a homogeneous color. Handmade slags have pontils. Machine-made slags consist of a colored transparent glass with opaque white swirls.

SOLID CORE - a handmade swirl with a series of bands in the center running from pontil to pontil that are spaced so closely together that no clear space remains between each band.

STEELIE - a marble made out of steel that can be either solid or hollow.

STRIAE - elongated imperfections in glass caused by temperature differences or unequal density of the materials used. Striae are not fractures.

SULPHIDE - objects made of china clay and supersilicate of potash that are inserted into a transparent glass sphere.

SWIRL - either a handmade marble with bands or strands running continuously unbroken from pontil to pontil, or a machine-made marble that is manufactured by injecting one or more colors into a base stream of glass.

TARGET - the marble in a game that was shot at by the shooter. Tournament regulations set the size at 5/8".

TAW - derived from alleytor; a prized shooter made of semiprecious stone, usually agate.

TRANSITIONAL - early machine-made marbles that were made partly by hand and partly by machine. Usually the glass was gathered by hand onto a punty and held over the machine. As the molten glass dripped down to the machine, a worker would snip off the proper amount and allow it to fall into the machine to be formed. The marble usually has one pontil.

BIBLIOGRAPHY

Allen, Shirley "Windy." *The Game of Marbles*. Marble King Inc., 1975.

Barrett, Marilyn. *Aggies, Immies, Shooters, and Swirls: The Magical World of Marbles*. Boston: Little, Brown and Company, 1994.

Baumann, Paul. *Collecting Antique Marbles*. Wallace-Homestead Book Co., 1994.

Block, Mark. *Contemporary Marbles and Related Art Glass*. Atglen, Pennsylvania: Schiffer Publishing, 2000.

Block, Robert. *Marbles: Identification and Price Guide*. Atglen, Pennsylvania: Schiffer Publishing, 2002.

_____. *Marbles Illustrated*. Atglen, Pennsylvania: Schiffer Publishing, 1999.

_____. *Pictorial Guide to Marbles*. Atglen, Pennsylvania: Schiffer Publishing, 2002.

Block, Stanley. "Marbles-Playing for Fun and for Keeps." *The Encyclopedia of Collectibles – Lalique to Marbles*. Time-Life Publications, 1983.

_____, editor. *Marble Mania*. Atglen, Pennsylvania: Schiffer Publishing, 1999.

_____. *Antique Sulphide Marbles*. Atglen, Pennsylvania: Schiffer Publishing, 2000.

_____. *Antique Swirl Marbles*. Atglen, Pennsylvania: Schiffer Publishing, 2001.

_____. *Antique End of Day Marbles*. Atglen, Pennsylvania: Schiffer Publishing, 2002.

Boy Scouts of America. *Cub Scout Sports: Marbles*. 1984.

Carskadden, Jeff, and Richard Gartley. *Chinas: Hand-painted Marbles of the Late 19th Century*. McClain Printing Co., 1990.

Carskadden, Jeff, and Mark Randall. "The Christensen Agate Company, Cambridge, Ohio (1927-1933)." *Muskingum Annals*, Volume 4, 1987.

Castle, Larry, and Marlowe Peterson. *The Guide to Machine-Made Marbles*. Utah Marble Connection, Inc., 1992.

Chevat, Richard. *The Marble Book*. Workman Publishing Company, 1996.

Degenhart, Paperweight & Glass Museum. *Reflection, Guernsey County Glass – 1883-1987*. Self-published, 1989.

Dickson, Paul. "Marbles." *Smithsonian*, April 1988.

Ferretti, Fred. *The Great American Marble Book*. Workman Press, 1983.

Grist, Everett. *Antique & Collectible Marbles*. Collector Books, 1992.

_____. *Big Book of Marbles*. Collector Books, 1994.

_____. *Machine-Made and Contemporary Marbles*. 1995.

Hardy, Roger, and Claudia Hardy. *The Complete Line of Akro Agate*. Self-published.

http://www.marblecollecting.com

http://www.akromarbles.com

Ingram, Clara. *The Collectors Encyclopedia of Antique Marbles*. Collector Books, 1972.

Levine, Shar. *A Marble Players Guide*. Sterling Publications, 1998.

Marble Collectors' Society of America. *Marble-Mania*. Quarterly newsletter. Published since 1976.

Morrison, Mel, and Carl Terrison. *Marbles – Identification and Price Guide*. Self-published, 1968.

Randall, Mark. *Marbles as Historical Artifacts*. Marble Collectors' Society of America, 1979.

Runyon, Cathy. *Knuckles Down! A Guide to Marble Play*. Right Brain Publishing Co., 1985.

Stanley, Mary Louise. *A Century of Glass Toys*. Forward's Color Productions, date unknown, early 1970s.

Taber, Ed. *The Klutz Book of Marbles*. Klutz Press, 1989.

Webb, Dennis. *Greenberg's Guide to Marbles*. Greenberg Publishing Co., Second Edition, 1994.

INDEX